# BERLIT.

C000242929

# COSTA DORADA
# and
# TARRAGONA

- A ✅ in the text denotes a highly recommended sight
- A complete A-Z of practical information starts on p.115
- Extensive mapping throughout: on cover flaps and in text

Printed in Switzerland by Weber SA, Bienne.

2nd edition (1995/1996)

**Although we make every effort to ensure the accuracy of the information in this guide, changes do occur. If you have any new information, suggestions or corrections to contribute, we would like to hear from you. Please write to Berlitz Publishing at the above address.**

| | |
|---|---|
| Text: | Paul Murphy |
| Editors: | Donald Greig, Sarah Hudson |
| Photography: | Paul Murphy |
| Layout: | Suzanna Boyle |
| Cartography: | MicroMap |
| | (p.115 *Falk* Falk-Verlag, Hamburg) |
| Thanks to: | Iberia Airline for their assistance in the preparation of this guide. |

Cover photograph:     Tamarit Castle, Tamarit: © The Image Bank

# CONTENTS

# The Costa Dorada and Tarragona

The Costa Dorada takes its name from those fine, golden (*daurada*) beaches that stretch almost continuously for over 240km (150 miles) along this calm Mediterranean shoreline. Technically the Costa Dorada begins in the south at the Ebro Delta and ends some 16km (10 miles) south of Sitges, where the Costa Garraf begins. This continues north as the Costa del Barcelona, before becoming the Costa del Maresme. This guide covers the region from the Ebro Delta up to and including the Maresme.

The Costa Dorada forms the southern shore of Catalonia, a large, autonomous (though not independent) part of Spain which stretches north to the French border and far west across the Pyrenees.

Catalonia is different to the rest of Spain, not least in its language. Those strange-looking and seemingly unpronounceable words with the x's that you'll see on street signs and menus are in Catalan. Whereas southern Spain was historically influenced by the Moors, the north of the country has always looked towards Europe. Andalucians may dance the fiery *flamenco*, but Catalans hold hands in a circle for the stately, measured *sardana*. Spanish traditions mean less here; the *siesta* is largely eschewed in favour of work, or an active lunch-break; menfolk are generally less macho, and women are now embarking on careers. Notably also, bullfighting is not a Catalan pastime. Catalans like to go their own way, and they defend their right to do so with a passion; just talk to them about Catalan history, or food, attend any fiesta, or watch a Barcelona football match in a crowded bar, and you'll soon see (or hear) the independent spirit for which the whole area is renowned.

The major metropolis of Catalonia is Barcelona. This lively, fashionable city boasts a fascinating Gothic Quarter, **5**

*The siesta is becoming just a memory in Barcelona – apparently not so in Vilassar de Mar!*

Roman legacy includes some of the finest monuments surviving from this period. Walk around the city walls, stroll under the great aqueduct, look down upon the once-bloody amphitheatre, and admire the museums and mosaics – Roman history comes alive in old *Tarraco*. There's also a fascinating mediaeval quarter here, and at its heart, one of Spain's finest cathedrals.

Tarragona offers more than history, though, from its lively Rambla to excellent beaches and good restaurants. Best of all, if you want to avoid other holidaymakers, it is relatively undiscovered.

One consequence of this is the shortage of good medium-priced accommodation (which is the city's only real drawback). Salou provides a good solution, however, and offers masses of affordable holiday

over 40 museums, art from antiquity to Gaudí and Miró, and restaurants and nightlife to rival any of the best in Europe. What's more, it is also a booming economic centre, producing almost 20 percent of Spain's industrial output.

There is, however, another main city on the Costa Dorada relatively unknown to international tourism. During Roman times, Tarragona was the most influential city on the whole of **6** the Iberian Peninsula. Now its accommodation a mere 10-15-minute bus ride away. Better still might be Cambrils, the salubrious neighbour of Salou, a charming fishing-port turned resort which is justly famous all over Catalonia for its fish restaurants.

You'll find the food is good all along the coast. Fish and seafood are nearly always the speciality on the menu, from exotic *paellas* and stews to simple grilled fish, served with Tarragona's uniquely delicious *romesco* sauce (see p.111).

The Costa Dorada is also renowned for its wines. Just north of Tarragona lies one of Spain's finest wine-producing areas, the Penedés. Here too are the *bodegas* which produce Spain's famous sparkling *cava*. A trip to the ancient market town of Vilafranca del Penedés and then to a *cava* producer makes for an excellent day out.

Further inland is the 10th-century Benedictine monastery of Montserrat – a must, not just for its religious trappings,

*Garraf, near Sitges, a neat resort with a good, sandy beach.*

but also for its seclusion and magical mountain setting.

The 12th-century Cistercian monasteries of Santes Creus and Poblet, meanwhile, conjure up the authentic atmosphere of an altogether different period. Alternatively, if you want the peace and quiet of nature without any man-made diversions, head south to the Ebro Delta, a wild and wonderful wetland where flamingos roost and rice is still gathered in the traditional way.

Don't miss a trip to Sitges either. It's the most complete resort on the Costa Dorada and is famous for letting its hair down, particularly at Carnival time – but then any fiesta round here is worth attending.

Finally, a word of warning on prices. Since Spain's integration into the EC, it has ceased to be one of Europe's bargain destinations. There's still plenty of good value, but don't be surprised if prices are not as low as they used to be.

# A Brief History

The first people to inhabit Catalonia were Paleolithic hunters who left their mark through cave paintings at Ulldecona, south of the Ebro Delta. Neolithic and Bronze Age relics have also turned up in the region around Tarragona, which was apparently predominantly used for cattle-rearing and agricultural purposes.

The Greeks and Phoenicians brought commerce and culture to Catalonia, while the Carthaginians are said to have given Barcelona its original name, *Barcino*, in honour of the general Hamilcar Barca, father of the legendary Hannibal. Barca established his base in 237 BC and moved south, establishing a further stronghold at Tarragona and subjugating much of the country

*O*ptimus' delicate Sepulchral Mosaic is in Tarragona's Palaeo Christian Museum, housing superb art from the 4th century.

south of the Ebro Delta. His son, Hannibal, was to lose it all some 20 years later, however, when he provoked the Romans into entering Catalonia to embark upon the Second Punic War.

## The Spanish Roman Empire

It was Cneus Cornelius Scipio who first established a military praesidium at *Tarraco* (Roman

for Tarragona) and used it as a base from where he could attack Hannibal's forces. After 16 years of battle, Scipio's army was victorious and Hannibal fled into exile (later to commit suicide).

*Tarraco* was established as the capital of the new region, and continued to be a military centre of command, directing operations to annex all Hispanic territories to the Roman Empire. It was considered an ideal point not only as it was the main port on the sea routes between the Italian peninsula and the Hispanic north-east, but it also held an advanced position for penetrating both east and south. Last, but not least, it enjoyed a very pleasant climate.

It took almost 200 years to subdue the native tribes in the central and northern areas of present-day Spain, but eventually the Roman country was to prosper. Tarragona enjoyed particular prominence during the reign of Julius Caesar, who called the settlement *Colonia Julia Victrix Triumphalis* to commemorate his victories.

In 27 BC, under the reign of Emperor Augustus, the Iberian

Peninsula was reorganized to form *Tarraconensis* (covering north, north-west and central Spain), *Lusitania* (approximating to modern Portugal) and *Baetica* (southern Spain), and *Tarraco* became capital of the largest Roman province within Hispania. This region coined its own money and boasted two forums (one for the local council, one for the provincial) and a number of monuments, many of which still remain.

The vaults for the circus tiers, the magnificent aqueduct, the Roman amphitheatre, and the sturdy Praetori build-

ing all attest to the importance of *Tarraco* at the height of the Spanish Roman Empire. Of course, they also left their language, with Latin forming the basis of the dialect, Catalan.

Tarragona was also to be an important centre in the spread of Christianity across the region. There is a strong belief that St Paul preached in the city, and in AD 259, the bishop of *Tarraco* became the earliest Christian martyr on the peninsula when he was burned alive in the amphitheatre. Some four centuries later, this gruesome event was commemorated by the erection of a Visigothic basilica on the site, the ruins of which still remain.

## Visigoths and Moors

By the 5th century, Rome's grip had slackened and Spain was besieged by the Vandals

*C*astles aren't too common in this part of Spain, so this one at Castellet is well worth the short detour from Sitges.

*The Gothic chapel of San Bartolomé – surprisingly not in a church, but in the beautiful Museo Maricel at Sitges.*

and the Visigoths. Although Barcelona and Tarragona were sacked, the Visigoths, who had been allies of Rome, did establish a sort of civilized order, which lasted until AD 711. In the same year, a Moorish army was foolishly invited into the country and, not content with the role of mere mercenaries, the Muslim forces assailed the entire Iberian Peninsula and Catalonia was briefly overrun.

However, the Moors were defeated beyond the Pyrenees by Charlemagne's Franks in AD 732, and withdrew to the south without leaving anything of great note.

Under the patronage of the Franks, Barcelona gained its independence in AD 878, but Tarragona, sacked, then abandoned by the Moors, was not to be reclaimed by Christian forces until the 11th century.

## Catalonia's Golden Age

In the early Middle Ages, Catalonia prospered. It received its own constitution and, with expedient marriages, managed to form unions with Provence and Aragon. Expansion overseas took off in 1229 when Jaume I set sail from Salou to dislodge the Moors from the Balearics. His son, Pedro III, was later to add Sicily to the growing empire.

By the 14th century, lands controlled included two dukedoms of Greece, Sardinia and Corsica, and for a time the kingdom of Catalonia was the most powerful in the Mediterranean. This too was an era of bold architecture, of which the Cathedrals of Tarragona and Barcelona, and the Cistercian abbeys of Poblet and Santes Creus are fine testament.

## Hard Times

The discovery of the Americas by Columbus in 1492 was to prove disastrous for Catalonia. The Mediterranean lost some of its importance as a trading zone, while the southern ports swiped the rich transatlantic business.

Worse was still to come. In 1494, administrative power was given to Castilian Spain, and the church Inquisition, with its policy of total Jewish expulsion, was imposed. The Jewish population of Barcelona completely disappeared, while Tarragona's was hugely reduced. During the next century Madrid replaced Barcelona as the capital of Spain.

During the 17th century, Catalonia was a troubled land, rebelling against King Philip IV and siding with Spain's enemy, France. In 1652, after 12 years of fighting, Barcelona gave in and renewed its allegiance to Spain. But 50 years later Catalonia again took the wrong side, this time in the War of the Spanish Succession, and was punished. Both the Catalan parliament and the language were banned.

In the second half of the 18th century, Charles III rescued the region from a trading slump by opening up profitable trade routes with Latin **13**

America. Tarragona prospered as a major wine blending and export centre, the profits from which were ploughed back in to a now burgeoning Catalan textile trade.

## War and Peace

For Catalonia and Spain, the 19th century seemed to be one long series of wars, starting with the War of Independence in 1808 and ending in 1898 with the Spanish-American War. Yet despite them, Catalan industry developed ahead of the rest of Spain. The country's first railway was built in

1848 along the Costa del Maresme, from Barcelona to Mataró, and then extended to Tarragona. Towards the end of the century, the *cava* industry began bubbling in earnest, and Barcelona expanded rapidly.

The century finished with general disillusionment as to the ability and role of the royalty, but, with no democratic structure to replace it, the 20th century ushered in increasing working-class political dissatisfaction and a failing economy. Confusion, disorder and even anarchy were growing. King Alfonso XIII was succeeded by General Primo de

### Modernisme

Despite the uncertain political times of the late 19th century, the arts were flourishing, with the movement known as *Modernisme* (the Spanish form of *art nouveau*) at the fore.

A rebellion against the rigid form and colourless stone and plaster of the classical architecture that had replaced Gothic, the style thrived (and has subsequently been preserved) in Catalonia, and particularly in Barcelona. Gaudí's Barcelona works are legendary, but elsewhere in the province you will also see many fine examples of this school, from grand lines and designs on the most elegant public buildings to simple adornments gracing humbler homes.

Rivera in 1923 in a military *coup*, but he brought no respite to the country's ailing condition, and after seven years the general fell. Elections in 1931 brought the Republican party to power and Catalonia briefly won back its independence.

## The Franco Years

The following five years were scarred by violent demonstrations and strikes until 1936, when General Francisco Franco led a military insurrection which soon became a bitter and bloody civil war. Catalonia remained fiercely Republican whilst Barcelona was bombed by Italian fighters.

The bloodiest battle of all was at the Ebro near Tortosa (see p.59). Barcelona fell in 1939, and Catalonia was reabsorbed into Spain. Within two months the war had ended, having claimed 750,000 lives. Once again Catalonia's autonomy was lost and its language was banned.

After keeping Spain out of the Second World War, Franco was assisted in the rebuilding of the economy post-war by the advent of mass tourism and the 1953 American Aid plan (in exchange for land for airforce bases). He died in 1975, but not without ensuring his successor would be Juan Carlos, grandson of Alfonso XIII.

## Modern Times

After an initial period following Francoist policies, Juan Carlos realized that only a democracy would satisfy the people, and in 1976 the first elections for 40 years were held. Catalonia was also given back its autonomy.

As if to remind the world that Spain is still a fledgling democracy, another *coup* was repelled by the king in 1981. In 1986 Spain joined the EC, and since then has benefited enormously from investment. Today Barcelona has become one of the fastest-growing of western Europe's economies, a status enhanced by the success of the 1992 Olympic Games. Meanwhile, Catalonia remains without doubt one of Spain's most exciting regions to visit. **15**

# Where to Go

## The Costa del Maresme

The area of the Costa del Maresme stretches some 38km (24 miles) from Mataró, north of Barcelona, to the Rio Tordero, where the Costa Brava begins. *Maresme* means a low-lying coastal region susceptible to flooding, and it could hardly be in more complete contrast to the rugged cliffs of the neighbouring coast.

Here the beaches are long and narrow, and often divided from the towns whose name they bear by the railway and busy N11 road which run parallel to the coast. (To reach the beach you first have to find the subway!) In many places, the Costa del Maresme is less developed than the Costa Dorada, and is almost exclusively the retreat of Spanish holidaymakers. The train is also a boon to anyone who wants to avoid the famous traffic jams. At weekends and during the summer holidays, the N11 is bumper-to-bumper with frustrated Barceloneses.

The first resort of note, **Vilassar de Mar**, has a spacious beach, but it is the small town itself that is really of interest. Look for the well-preserved,

*V*ilassar de Mar boasts fine functional structures (left, a watchtower) and ornamental architecture (Modernist mansions, right).

16th-century **watch-tower** on the main road. This is just one of many along this coast and is a legacy of the days when the inhabitants lived in fear of raiding corsairs. Close by is a group of fine **19th-century houses** which carry flamboyant hallmarks of *Modernisme* (see p.14); these are good examples of the type of building typical to this area.

With a population of some 100,000, **Mataró** is by far the biggest town on the Maresme. It's not a resort, but it does have a good beach, and you might wish to explore the old part of this once-walled town. The **basilica of Santa Maria** is the most notable of several baroque buildings here. In addition, you can't help but notice the fruit and vegetable crops by the roadside – thanks to the fertile soil, the Maresme region is known as 'the vegetable garden of Barcelona'.

If you enjoy watching sleek new yachts and powerboats, drop in at Mataró's new marina, where there is berthing for over 1,000 vessels. In fact, this small stretch of the Maresme

*From this clifftop vantage-point above delightful Callella, you'll look over the splendid beach to watch the watersports.*

is highly popular with the yachting fraternity; El Masnou, Premiá de Mar, Llavaneres (north of Mataró), and Arenys De Mar also boast sizeable marinas.

Although there's a pleasant beach at Sant Andreu de Llavaneres, it's worth continuing a little further to the more **18** up-market **Caldes d'Estrac** (also known as Caldetes) for a leisurely stop. Lavish turn-of-the-century Catalan seaside villas and swish restaurants line the palm-fringed *passeig* *maritim* (promenade) backed by green hills. The beach has been divided into sections by stone breakwaters which form small crescents of sand. The Romans were the first to bathe here, though not in the sea, but in the same 39°C (102°F) mineral waters which also led the Edwardians to establish a resort here.

**Arenys de Mar** has been a seafaring town since the 16th century, and although the new marina is now an international focus of attention for regattas, the old port remains characterful and offers a good supply of fish restaurants. If you want to eat where the fisherman go, try the Cofadría de Pescadores San Telmo. There is a good beach next door where you can sleep off your fish lunch, and the town itself, dominated by its long, wide, tree-lined Rambla, is well worth a visit. On the Rambla is a fine parish church renowned for its elaborate (some say over-elaborate) baroque altarpiece. Wander as well through the narrow, old streets and also visit the small **Museu Mares de la Punta**, which is reputed to be one of the best fine lace museums in Europe. Another local speciality is *Calisay*, a famous brand of orange liqueur which is made in the centre of town. Enquire at the tourist office for details of times of guided distillery tours.

**Canet de Mar** is a straightforward seaside resort on the N11 road. It calls itself the *Vila Catalana del Modernisme* (the Catalan town of Modernism, see p.14) and claims some 60 Modernist buildings. The centrepiece is the **Casa Museu,** the former home (and now a museum) of Lluís Domènech i Montaner, who lived all his life in Canet de Mar. Well-known as a follower of the school of *Modernisme*, he is most renowned for his design of the stunning Palau de la Música Catalana in Barcelona – arguably the city's greatest work of its kind.

**Santa Pol de Mar** is probably the most charming village along the Costa del Maresme. Narrow, winding streets lead up to a **mediaeval monastery** and an ancient watch-tower **19**

perched high above the beach. Down below, you can change for the beach in Victorian bathing huts, rent an old-fashioned deck chair with arm supports, and sink into a beach scene which, apart from the style of the bathing costumes, has changed little this century.

The king of the costa is without doubt **Calella** (also called Calella de la Costa so as to distinguish it from Calella de Palafrugell on the Costa Brava). Driving to it from the south, the approach is distinguished by a **lighthouse**, quite remote from the seashore, high on a rocky cliff above the road. Opposite is a lay-by where curious spectators peer down some 18-24m (60-80ft) at the prettiest and smallest of Calella's beaches. (The beach is also popular with naturists, which may of course be the reason for the crowds above.)

As the cliff-hugging road swings to the left, the vast expanse of Calella's **main beach** is revealed on the opposite side of the road in all its panoramic glory. The vast, wide, golden sands are neatly punctuated by high-tech beach bar awnings, and during the summer you'll find they are chock-a-block with truly dedicated sunbathers.

The resort generally bustles with tourist development and there is now little left of the old settlement. The **Municipal Museum**, housed in a fine old building, is worth a look, as is the pretty church. On your way to the beach, by the railway lines, there is still some fine typical Catalan seaside-resort architecture.

Callella sprawls south along the coast and finally collides with **Pineda de Mar** and **Santa Susanna**. Pineda has a particularly good beach.

The final town of any size on the Costa del Maresme is **Malgrat de Mar**. With its 3km (2 miles) of beach, it is popular with both Spanish and foreign tourists alike, but as an industrial town it holds less general appeal than some of its neighbours. Nearby are two notable attractions: **Marineland** (see p.98) and **Castell Mediaeval**.

# Barcelona

Barcelona is a sophisticated city where the creative energy of modern Europe and the relaxed pleasures of the Mediterranean meet in happy union. It may be Spain's second city, but it is very definitely a capital, though now of a culture rather than a country.

Go straight to the famous **Rambla** – half promenade and half bazaar – to catch the feeling of the city. There's a bustle and energy here which is unmatched almost anywhere else in Europe. The Rambla is also a good point of orientation. At the bottom is the seaport, to the east is the cathedral and the **Barri Gòtic** (the Gothic/Mediaeval Quarter, see p.25), at the top end is the 19th-century city, famous for its Modernist architecture, and to the west rises **Montjuïc**, hub of the dazzling 1992 Olympics.

Barcelona's avenues, broad and leafy, boast plazas, statues and fountains at the main intersections. Few skyscrapers intrude on the human scale of the city profile. The buildings

*The Telefèric de Montjuïc offers breathtaking views of Barcelona – from funfair to Gaudí's amazing Sagrada Família church.*

which leave an impression are usually banks; almost as numerous as the bars, they are a reminder that for all its southern European flair, this is also a city of big business.

If you only have a couple of days to see the city, or if you want to get an easy introduction without the restrictions of a coach tour, then jump aboard the **Bus Turistic** (mid-June to September only). This is an excellent hop-on hop-off service which takes in the most interesting parts of the city. Services are frequent and once you've seen all that you want of a certain place, you never have to wait long for the next bus. The bus fare also entitles you to free cable-car, funicular and tram rides and to discounts on admission to several attractions – pick up a leaflet from any tourist office. If you're coming from the general direction of Tarragona, it couldn't be easier, as the bus stops at Sants Station.

The first stop from Sants is **Montjuïc**. In 1992 the 'Hill of the Jews' was transformed into a new Mount Olympus as millions of television viewers thrilled to pictures of high-board divers perched spectacularly above the city at the open-air Olympic swimming pool. The hill is no stranger to big events. In 1929 it was the site of the International Exhibition, at which time the ornate fountains of the **Plaça d'Espanya** were created to grace the entrance. The gateway is also marked by two, huge brick columns modelled on St Mark's Campanile in Venice. Several large hangar-type halls, still used for commercial exhibitions, lead up to the **Palau Nacional**, domed like the US Capitol and dominating the skyline. This was the Spanish Pavilion in 1929 and now houses the **Museu d'Art de Catalunya**, containing one of the world's finest collections of mediaeval art.

There are so many attractions on Montjuïc alone that it would be easy to spend several days here. Chief among them is the **Poble Espanyol** (Spanish Village) where you can see the whole of Spain in a couple of hours. The village is

# BARCELONA METRO

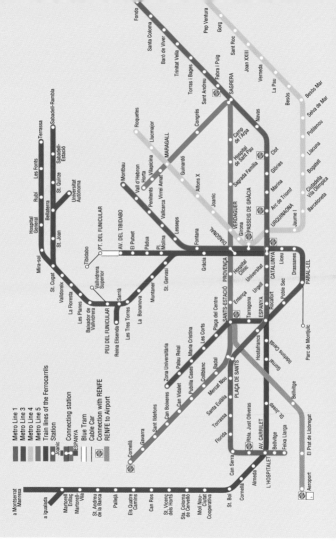

**Legend:**
- Metro Line 1
- Metro Line 3
- Metro Line 4
- Metro Line 5
- Train lines of the Ferrocarrils
- Station
- Joanic — Connecting station
- ESPANYA — Blue Tram
- Cable Car
- Connection with RENFE
- RENFE to Airport

a showcase of the country's various regions, each of which are represented by miniature replicas of houses, churches, fountains, plazas and palaces. There are 115 of them in total, interspersed with shops, restaurants, tapas bars and artisans' workshops. It may not be the real thing, but it's a good crash course to the delights of the country, while the audiovisual 'Barcelona Experience' provides an easy introduction to the city.

If you are in search of more cerebral diversions, there are plenty of other museums and galleries on Montjuïc. In particular, don't miss the witty, abstract art of the highly-rated **Fundació Joan Miró**.

Take the bus to the cable-car, the **Telefèric de Montjuïc**, which takes you on a breathtaking ride high above the Olympic swimming pool and the city skyline to the fairground of the **Parc d'Atraccions de Montjuïc**. At the summit of the hill is the impressive 17th-century **Castell de Montjuïc**, which houses a military museum.

The beginning of the Rambla is marked by the statue of Christopher Columbus, on top of his 50m (164ft) **Monument a Colom**. Leave the famous street for a little while longer, however, and take a look out over the waterfront.

A replica of the *Santa María*, Columbus' flagship, is berthed near the fleet of boats that tour the harbour. There is also cable-car here, swinging above the harbour to the colourful dockside area, **La Barceloneta**, famous for its fish restaurants. If you are at all interested in seafaring history, do not miss the **Museu Marítim** (next to the Monument a Colom), which chronicles over seven centuries of shipbuilding in Barcelona.

**La Rambla** stretches nearly 1.5km (1 mile) up a gentle incline to the very hub of the city, the **Plaça de Catalunya**. Although it changes its name seamlessly five times from top to bottom, the character and locals do alter throughout.

The lower stretches are the seediest, with the **Barrí Xino** (Chinatown), to the left, best avoided by night. A little further along and just off the Rambla is the **Palau Güell**, a splendid, fortress-like mansion built by Gaudí in 1885 for his principal patron, the textile tycoon Count Eusebi Güell.

On the opposite side of the Rambla is the handsome, but decayed **Plaça Reial**. Until recently, this arcaded square was the notorious haunt of down-and-outs, but is now regaining its fashionable image of former years. Also on this stretch of the Rambla you'll start to encounter street entertainers: musicians, fire-eaters, human statues, jugglers, and a host of other eccentric performers.

The next building of note is the **Gran Teatre del Liceu** – a monument of the Catalan *Renaixença* period – as plush inside today as when it opened in 1847. Across the street is the venerable **Café del'Opera** – a good spot to stop for some refreshment.

The heart of the Rambla is the **Pla de la Boquería** – its 19th-century covered market, known as **La Boquería**, is a city highlight. Huge, lovingly-arranged mounds of fruit, vegetables, sausages, meat, poultry, seafood, herbs, spices and sweetmeats form a cornucopian mosaic under the high-ceilinged, ironwork naves. It opens at dawn but closes mid-afternoon, so time your visit accordingly.

The next part of the Rambla is famous for its flowers and is one of the most photographed scenes in the city. The blossoms give way to birds and their vendors and the Rambla finishes at Plaça de Catalunya.

If you step off the Rambla about half-way along and walk east for a short distance, you will find yourself in the **Barri Gòtic** – the oldest part of town. This is an atmospheric area of narrow alleyways and old buildings, many of which have been regenerated as museums, hotels or restaurants. You'll find the best bits in a well-preserved concentration of mediaeval architecture clustered around the **Catedral de Santa Eulalia**. It's not hard to find this huge, imposing, time-blackened building. It was begun in the 13th century,  **25** though its Gothic façade was not finished until 1892. Try not to miss the beautiful cloister.

Next door is the **Palau Reial** (Royal Palace), famed as the place where Columbus met Ferdinand and Isabella in 1493 to report what he had found in the New World.

There are also two excellent museums here: the **Museu d'Història de la Ciutat** (Museum of the History of the City), in a rebuilt 15th-century mansion, and a must if you want an historical perspective on the city; and the **Museu Frederic Marés**, a wonderful eclectic collection of religious objects, art and miscellany.

Just outside the Barri Gòtic is Barcelona's most popular museum, the **Museu de Picasso**. Devoted to the works of the great artist, it occupies a splendid mediaeval palace in the Carrer de Montcada, one of the mediaeval city's best-preserved streets. Unfortunately, you won't see Picasso's greatest works in here, and there are few Cubist pieces, but it is nonetheless an excellent collection.

Continue south along the Carrer de Montcada to reach one of the city's finest churches, **Santa Maria del Mar**. As the name suggests, at this point you are almost back on the waterfront.

Just to the east of here is the **Ciutadella**, named after a prison erected by the French in 1714, and torn down with much glee in 1869. It's now a lovely, mature park, famous as the site of **Barcelona Zoo**, and home to Snowflake (the albino gorilla), performing dolphins and a killer whale.

From the Rambla, the Bus Turistic continues its journey north through the modern part of the city which is known as **L'Eixample** ('the expansion', built largely between 1860 and 1920). This district is famous for its Modernist architecture, and the buildings not to miss are all on Passeig de Gràcia. Note in particular: no. 35, **Casa Lleó Morera**, by Domènech i Montaner; no. 41, **Casa Amatller** by Puig i Cadafalch; no. 43, **Casa Batlló** by Gaudí; and no. 92, **Casa Milà** (also known as La Pedrera) by

*T*win Peaks – two of the crazily, magically decorated spires of Gaudí's Sagrada Família church.

Gaudí. The latter two are both extraordinary buildings, with all of Gaudí's inventive, surrealist hallmarks.

For more of the master of *Modernisme*, rejoin the bus to the city's most famous landmark, the church of **Sagrada Família** (Holy Family). No matter how many pictures you have seen of this unfinished masterpiece, you won't be disappointed by the reality.

The basic shape is firmly rooted in Barcelona's Gothic tradition, but no other Gothic church has stonework which drips like melted candlewax, or sculptures of snails, vines and tortoises, or 100m (330ft) towers that resemble perforated cigars.

An elevator and steps take you all the way up to view the detail on the amazing towers, including Gaudí's famous 'broken-plate mosaics'.

The church is unfinished, and as Gaudí's plans were destroyed during the Civil War, no-one knows what his exact intentions were. Work continues, but at a snail's pace, and it seems unlikely that Sagrada Família will be finished in the foreseeable future.

More of Gaudí's work can be found north of Sagrada Família at the **Parc Güell**. His patron, Count Güell, intended to create a community of villas here within the 2.4ha (6-acre) park, and in 1900 gave Gaudí **27** *carte blanche* to produce an original design. The result is a compendium of the designer's most distinctive devices – dragons, drunken columns (86 of them supporting the roof of what was to have been the colony's covered market), a

*Try paella at Barcelona's Poble Espanyol. Spain's favourite dish is a visual and gastronomic treat.*

serpentine wall and tiled mosaic bench around a raised plaza, and mask-eyes as windows. However, the villa plan never took off, and the property became a popular family park in 1923. Here is also the house in which Gaudí lived for a while, which now serves as a museum.

If you get a bright, clear day and want a view of Barcelona that puts Montjuïc into a different perspective, catch the bus to **Tibidabo** and change onto the city's last tram service. The famous 1900-vintage **tramvia blau** (blue tram) takes you almost to the top of this 542m (1,778ft) peak overlooking Barcelona, then it's another 5-minute trip on the funicular to the top. There's a good amusement park here combining the best of old- and new-technology rides.

If you still have a desire to see religious buildings, the **Monestir de Pedralbes** (on the north-eastern edge of the city centre) boasts a superb Gothic church and a charming two-storey cloister. It is only open until 2pm.

A temple to an altogether different Spanish passion, although one that is hardly less devout, lies just south of here. The 120,000-seat **Camp Nou Stadium** is famous all over the footballing world as the home of **Barcelona FC**. Tours of both the ground and of the Museu del Futbol are becoming a major attraction.

All of the above mentioned sights can be seen on the **Bus Turistic** route. Catch the first and last shuttles and you can see a good number of them in a single day (although it's obviously a much better idea to spend at least one night here). Barcelona is famous for its choice of restaurants and tapas bars (see p.74), as well as its lively nightlife. The Barri Gòtic is an ideal place to stay, as it lies within easy walking distance of most of the entertainments.

Barcelona is connected to all Costa Dorada resorts by fast and frequent train services, and you would be well advised not to drive here unless you really have to, as the city is difficult to navigate.

# Barcelona to Tarragona

The industrial outskirts on the western side of Barcelona hold little interest for tourists, with the exception of the fact that this is the location of the city's **El Prat Airport**. There are also a number of campsites signposted off the main road, which are hidden behind the surrounding pine woods.

The first resort along the coast is **Castelldefells**, whose long, wide, sandy beach has proved popular amongst Barcelonan weekenders.

Beyond Castelldefells, take either the section of *autopista* called *Tunels de Garraf*, which cuts through the mountain, or follow the coast road, which winds its way along the cliffs, skirting a number of industrial installations before reaching the tiny resort of **Garraf**. This is a neat and tidy place, where old-fashioned green and white beach houses look out to sea, and smart villas blend into a mountainous backdrop. Continue along the coast road, and within a couple of kilometres **29**

of each other are two new marinas (*ports esportius*). The first, close to Garraf, is Port Ginesta, and the second, Port Aiguadolç, is a lively social centre, thanks to its proximity to Sitges.

Arriving in **Sitges** from the east is effectively like entering through the back door. The top

of the landmark church on the *Punta* (promontory) is visible but it is mostly hidden, and its back is towards you. The relatively quiet, small beach of San Sebastià stretches out for little more than 90m (300ft) and at its far end is the sturdy seawall which protects the promontory.

*Old Sitges (left), home to the mock-Gothic Palau Mar i Cel (detail, below).*

The old town, built around the *Punta*, is a delight. A narrow, cobbled street rises up to what appears to be a mediaeval palace, bearing the romantic name **Palau Mar i Cel** (usually contracted to Maricel), which means the 'palace of the sea and sky'. Joined above street level by walk-ways, and flaunting the gargoyles and galleries of a Notre Dame, the building is so tall that some of the narrow alleyways are permanently in shadow. Despite being Gothic in appearance, it was actually built in the 1920s (on the site of a 14th-century hospital) for American businessman and art **31** collector, Charles Deering. Inside, in a room with wonderful views out to sea through floor-to-ceiling windows, the **Museu Maricel** houses Deering's collection of paintings and *objets d'art* from around the world.

Also on the *Punta*, next door to the Museu Maricel, is the art and wrought-ironwork collection of Santiago Rusiñol (1861-1931), a leading exponent of *Modernisme* (see p.14) who named his studio-home **Cau Ferrat** (the 'iron lair') after his work. Here, other leading sculptors and painters of the day would meet, forging the beginnings of Sitges as a fashionable artists' and intellectuals' colony. Cau Ferrat holds more than just Rusiñol's splendid ironwork, however. Paintings by such masters as El Greco and Picasso, as well

### Castellet and L'Arboç

For a half-day break from the coast between Sitges and El Vendrell, take the E15 country road from north of Vilanova i la Geltrú. This picturesque road cuts through rolling countryside and vineyards, before rising up to the hamlet of **Castellet**. Here, a well-preserved, sturdy mediaeval castle commands a marvellous view over the lovely reservoir of Panta de Foix. From the restaurant on the main road just below, you can enjoy more panoramic views while sipping an aperitif.

Continue on the same road for 3km (2 miles) to the pretty village of **L'Arboç**. What makes this small community special is the number of interesting buildings here. Dominating the scene is a copy of Seville's famous Giralda Tower, while at the village entrance a mock castle is home to a *cava* winery. The most important historical structure is a Renaissance-style church, which contains a 12th-century Romanesque chapel, complete with fine, Gothic wall paintings. L'Arboç also boasts a renowned Modernist hospital structure, and there are plans to open a museum of lace in the village.

*S*itges is rich in Modernist flourishes. This sundial can be spotted on the seafront.

as beautiful ceramics and crystal are imaginatively displayed in one of Spain's most exquisite small museums.

At the very top of the hill is the **parish church**, built between the 16th and the 18th centuries. It may not be an architectural gem – in fact it is quite plain by day – but its dramatic setting more than compensates for any lack of aesthetic appeal, particularly at night when it is beautifully illuminated. As you stand and look down upon the 5km (3-mile) stretch of beach and the *Passeig Maritim* (promenade) of Sitges, much of the reason for the town's appeal becomes apparent, for this is one of those increasingly rare Spanish resorts that has not fallen victim to the excesses of 20th-century tourism.

The old town slopes inland from the church and tumbles down the narrow streets which culminate in the *Passeig Maritim*. Antique and art galleries, whitewashed houses, colourful local shops, a park where *sardanas* (see p.91) are regularly performed, enticing cafés, restaurants, and lively bars can all be found here.

Another good museum in Sitges is the **Museu Romàntic**, a mansion lavishly decorated in 19th-century style and full of interesting contemporary objects, including clocks, working music boxes, and a renowned collection of dolls. **33**

The far end of the town is quiet. Here wealthy Barcelonan families enjoy tranquillity behind lofty, trimmed hedges. It is the young, trendy Barceloneses who make Sitges such a fashionable and lively spot. Just take a walk along the *Calle 1er de Maig* (1st May) to feel the atmosphere. Since the 1960s, a sizeable and semi-permanent gay population has brought particular verve, colour and humour to Sitges. The fiestas here are among the most colourful outside Barcelona, with **Carnaval** being particularly outrageous (see p.95). At the other end of the spectrum, however, Sitges is also known for its **Corpus Christi** celebrations (see p.96).

To complete the picture, this all-round resort also offers good watersports facilities and a fine golf course. Meanwhile, at San Pere de Ribes, 3km (2 miles) north, the region's high rollers converge on the **Gran Casino de Barcelona**.

A few miles along the coast, the city of **Vilanova i La Geltrú** also has an extensive sand beach, but is less developed than Sitges. Away from the beach, a bustling network of narrow streets is home to a population of some 45,000. This is a workaday Spanish town, but don't be put off by its rather unprepossessing appearance. If you don't want to venture into its maze of streets and alleyways, there are still the seafront and three good museums to explore.

The first two museums are just off the main Tarragona road. The grand *fin-de-siècle* Modernist building of the **Museu Balaguer** is clearly distinguishable from the road. It is devoted mainly to 19th- and 20th-century paintings by Catalan artists, but there are some Old Masters as well. A few yards away is a **railway museum** which will delight trainspotters of all ages. It's not so much 'hands on' as 'clamber on'. Several lovingly-restored old-time locomotives are displayed in engine sheds or out in the open air.

The **Casa Papiol Museum** is tucked away in the town's backstreets (ask for a map at the helpful Museu Balaguer).

*S*plendid examples from the Age of Steam can be viewed at Vilanova i La Geltrú's highly rated railway museum.

A sister building to the Museu Romàntic in Sitges (see p.33), it is an 18th-century mansion re-creating Spanish noble life.

Down at the seafront (where you'll find the tourist office) is one of Catalonia's busiest **fishing ports**. Here, large international vessels jostle for space with traditional, small Spanish fishing boats. Close by, the **Castillo de La Geltrú** is a much-restored 13th-century building where ancient artefacts are exhibited alongside modern Catalan art.

The coast west of Vilanova is lined with a succession of family seaside resorts. Each is well-developed (mainly with **35**

*Cool Cats can be hired at most of the beaches stretching west of Vilanova i La Geltrú.*

medium-rise apartments and hotels), and is small, neat and tidy, with long, clean golden beaches offering the usual facilities, including most watersports. In addition to this is the further good news that the beaches of Coma-ruga, Cunit, Calafell and Sant Salvador have all been awarded European blue flags.

The first of these resorts is **Cubelles**, where some of the beaches have been shaped by the tide into attractive crescents – perfect for safe swimming. The village also has an imposing 17th-century church. Neighbouring **Cunit** also has a good beach, stretching some 3km (2 miles), although divided by breakwaters.

Next is the lengthy shore of **Calafell**, the most developed of this group of resorts. The old part is dominated by the ruins of a sturdy-looking castle perched on what appears to be a volcanic outcrop. The town of Calafell peters out into Segur de Calafell, where there is a small marina.

With its ancient buildings, which include a mediaeval city gate, and a small Rambla, **El Vendrell** is the most distinctive of these coastal towns. It is also an important wine town and you will see fields of vines in the surrounding area. For sea and sand take the road for some 3km (2 miles) to the town's beach at Sant Salvador.

Finally in this small group is **Coma-ruga** (also written Comarruga), another well developed and fashionable resort with big hotels to complement its comfortable villas. Known as a spa and sporting centre, it also has a small marina and a beach stretching for over 4km (2.5 miles).

The N246 coast road stops at Coma-ruga and heads inland to pick up the busy N340 which continues east as the new coast route. This follows the Roman road, the Appian Way, and just beyond Coma-ruga is a reminder of those days. In the middle of the road stands a huge, triumphal arch known as the **Arc de Berà**. It's as tall as a three-storey building and has stood here since the 2nd century. Cars used to drive through it, but increased traffic dictates that they now

---

### Pablo Casals (1876-1973)

Born in El Vendrell in 1876, the cellist, Pablo (Pau) Casals, became one of the great musicians of this century (tirelessly continuing to perform well into his eighties), as well as being a champion of human rights and a staunch advocate of Catalan independence.

If you want to learn more about him, go along to the beach quarter of El Vendrell, Sant Salvador, where his old summer house is open to the public. In addition to musical memorabilia, the house holds a fine collection of Catalan art. Concerts are held periodically at the auditorium opposite.

go round it. Look out for the turn-off to **Roc Sant Gaietà**; the eponymous rock on which the village is built overlooks an attractive, unspoiled cove.

*The region from Barcelona to Tarragona is famous for its wines – look out for grape-picking from September onwards.*

**Torredembarra**, by contrast, is a busier resort. The beach here is broad and long and development is just starting to take off. The town, however, has been virtually untouched and has a very solid church and a fine, old castle in an endearing state of decay.

Next door is **Altafulla**, arguably the prettiest settlement between Tarragona and Sitges. This picturesque town of well-preserved pink, stone houses, many of which date from the 18th century, climbs steeply up narrow streets, towards the church and the 11th-century castle. En route is the town's modern art museum, housed in an historic old property.

Altafulla has a reasonable beach of the same name and close by is the excellent beach of **Tamarit**. A narrow track leads off the main road, wending through vegetable fields and a campsite, until it comes to the dramatic cliff-top Castle of Tamarit (not open to the public), built in the 11th century to defend the coast against the Moors. Below it you'll find the beach.

# Tarragona

Tarragona is best entered from the east along the old Vía Augusta, where ancient Roman roadside monuments whet the appetite for the historic city that is to come.

Continuing on our journey from the east, just off the main road is **El Médol**, the stone quarry which provided the raw materials for several of the Roman structures in Tarragona. The vertical quarry walls plunge down to a monolith known as **L'Agulla del Médol** (the Needle of Médol). Carved from the original rock, it was deliberately worked to indicate the depth of the excavations.

Note the type of stone here; you will see it later in a more polished state in the buildings of Tarragona.

Just a little further on, and at the very edge of the road, is the **Torre de los Escipiones** (Tower of the Scipios – two brothers who were important protagonists in early Roman military campaigns in Hispania). Little can be said with certainty about this immense, square funerary tower, but the figures still visible on the front of the monument are thought to represent Atis, an Eastern god of the funerary cult. The tower is probably a tomb and certainly at one time had a pyramidal top. Unfortunately

### Blood of Christ

If you've ever wondered where the wine that is used to celebrate Holy Communion comes from, the answer may well be Tarragona.

De Muller, the city's largest and most prestigious wine concern, have been specialist suppliers of altar wine for generations. Exporting organically produced white wine all over the world, they have been suppliers to the Vatican and many popes. In keeping with the changing taste of the market as a whole, altar wines have become less sweet in recent years.

*R*oman legacies in stone: the Pont del Diable (right) and the Head of Medusa in the Archaeological Museum (below).

the elements and other vagaries of time have taken their toll on its exterior.

Tarragona's most impressive Roman monument lies some 4km (2.5 miles) north of the centre of town, off the N240 Lleida (Lérida) road. If you thought that they didn't come much bigger than the towering Arc de Berà (see p.37) then you'd be wrong!

The **Pont del Diable** (the Devil's Bridge) is one of the greatest Roman structures still standing in Spain. A perfectly preserved double-decker aqueduct, it spans 217m (712ft), and has a total of 11 lower-storey and 25 upper-storey arches, the highest of which rise up to 27m (88ft) from the ground. It was built during the 1st century as part of a complex network of canals that supplied Tarragona with water,

and even today remains a tribute to the engineers of the day. Not only is the stonework in superb condition, but in places the original watercourse is still intact. The structure is also known as the aqueduct of 'Les Ferreres', which refers to the rusty, red water it carried over its arches.

Frustratingly, although you can see the aqueduct from the main road, access is not easy.

Look for a very narrow turning roughly ½km (¼ mile) south (Tarragona side) of the Restaurant Pont del Diable (you may well have to double back on yourself). It is unmarked, but there is a dilapidated entrance of sorts (take care when exiting from the busy main road). It is then a 10-minute walk to the bottom of the overgrown valley which the aqueduct spans (although it is not

in sight for most of the walk). A much better viewpoint is the one up above, off the A7 *autopista*, where sightseeing coaches pull over.

From the east, the Vía Augusta runs into the **Rambla Vella** (Old Rambla), which neatly divides the town in half. To the north is the old walled city, while parallel and to the south is the **Rambla Nova** (New Rambla) and the newer part of town. Before heading for the sights, relax at a café on the Rambla Nova and visit the very helpful tourist office, which will supply you with town maps and any other details you require.

##  The Roman city

The Romans landed in Tarragona (they called it *Tarraco*) during the 3rd century BC and rapidly established it as an important military and political headquarters. It grew to a population of 30,000, coined its own money and by 27 BC was the capital of Hispania Citerior (later *Tarraconensis*), the largest Roman province in Spain. During its period of occupation, a number of emperors lived here, including Augustus and Hadrian.

The best place to start getting acquainted with ancient *Tarraco* is the **Passeig Arqueològic** (Archaeological Promenade) which follows the top of the old city walls just north of the Rambla Vella. The entrance is at the Portal del Roser at the end of Avinguda Catalunya (your admission ticket also includes entrance to several other sights).

The **city walls** were built by the Romans immediately on their arrival. They rise up to 12m (39ft) high and in places are up to 6m (19ft) wide. This feat of engineering had a head start, however, since the initial settlers (peoples from the eastern Mediterranean) had somehow already placed in position titanic blocks, each weighing up to 35 tons, which the Romans promptly used as foundation stones.

The walk incorporates three solid Roman towers, a fine statue of the Emperor Augustus (presented to the city by

Mussolini), attractive gardens and a number of fine views. Don't be misled, however, into thinking the 'Greek Theatre' just down the hill is from antiquity; it's a modern municipal auditorium, built in 1970.

The British have also left their mark on the fortifications, their forces having positioned the outer walls in 1707 to secure the city during the War of Succession. The walk actually finishes outside the walls, but don't worry, to get back inside just keep the walls to your right and walk round the short distance to the **Portal de Sant Antoni**. The ornamentation is 18th century, but the gate is much older.

You are now entering a labyrinthine **mediaeval city**, very different from the Rambla Nova (although it has an obvious Mediterranean style), with flowerpots balanced on iron balconies, laundry drying in tall, dark, narrow streets, and canaries in cages on the walls. You will probably also see patriotic red- and yellow-striped Catalan flags draped from verandah railings.

If you can resist wandering at random through this fascinating part of town, stick to the Via Granada until you reach the Plaça del Rei (King's Square). The **Museu Arqueològic** here is a modern, well-designed exhibition of delicate mosaics (don't miss the Head of Medusa), and Roman and Spanish artefacts.

The ancient, roughly-hewn, tall, golden building adjacent to the museum is known as the **Pretori Romà** (Roman Praetorium), and is thought to have been part of the complex of original provincial administration buildings. During this period it also acquired the name of *Castell de Pilate* (Pilate's Castle), since it was traditionally known as the birthplace of Pontius Pilate. Pilate's father was praetor here before moving to Judea, where his son was to follow in his footsteps. The Emperor Augustus is also believed to have used the building as a palace, and so too did the mediaeval Aragonese kings, whence its other name, *Castell del Rei* (Kings' Castle). It is certainly Roman **43** in origin, though much restored in the Middle Ages, and it now houses the **Museu d'Història** (History Museum).

The contrast between the ancient, atmospheric shell of the building and the stylish, modern exhibition of artefacts telling the story of old Tarragona (captions in Spanish only) works well. Look out for the splendid Sarcophagus of Hippolytus, which was recovered from the sea in 1948. At the lowest level you can walk a short way along a tunnel which linked the castle with the **Roman Circus** (part of which was on the site where the Plaça de la Font now stands) and acted as supporting vaults for the Circus tiers. Just next door to the Pretori Romà are further remains of the Circus.

Walking from here towards the sea brings you to the hillside ruins of the Roman **amphitheatre**. Gladiators once fought here, and on this site, in AD 259, the first Christians on the peninsula were martyred by fire. A church, dedicated to their memory, was built

**44**

within the amphitheatre, but only its ruins remain today.

Three other important ancient sites, situated beyond the city walls, should also be mentioned before we turn again to mediaeval Tarragona.

Near the colourful central market – which is worth a visit in its own right – on Carrer Lleida, you will find the remains of Tarragona's local **Forum** (the city's Provincial Forum was set inside the city walls). There's not a lot left now: a few isolated columns and arches bear testimony to the once arcaded square which would have been filled with court rooms, temples, shops and other buildings.

The second site dates from towards the end of the Roman period, and is located on the western edge of the city centre. The **Necròpoli i Museu Paleocristià** (Necropolis and Palaeo-Christian Museum) is on the site of a cemetery for Tarragona's early Christians, and comprises a series of covered excavations. More than 2,000 graves have been unearthed here, and a museum displays

*A beautiful sarcophagus carving at the Palaeo-Christian Museum illustrates life during the late Roman period.*

the best of the finds. Naturally, it's not the cheeriest of places, but there are some good pieces in the museum, including fine sarcophagi. Perhaps best of all is the colourful 4th-century Optimus Sepulchral Mosaic, regarded as a masterpiece of early Christian art. Note too the unusual ivory doll which holds pride of place in an illuminated case. Fully articulated, it was found in a child's grave and dates from back in the 3rd century.

If you'd like to learn more about late Roman/early Christian ways of life and death, head north for 5km (3 miles) to Constanti, and in the village of **Centcelles** you will find a 4th-century villa and mausoleum. The mosaics on the cupola represent a deer hunt, the four seasons, and biblical stories, including Daniel in the Lion's Den and Jonah and the Whale. This may have been intended as the last resting place for Emperor Constans, who died in AD 350, and indeed some authorities claim that he is actually buried here.

## Mediaeval Tarragona

To return to the old city, re-enter by the side of the Pretori, and from the Praça del Rei take the Vía Santa Anna. Left is the **Museu d'Art Modern**, **45**

where, in a fine city mansion, the shock of the new contrasts well with the grace of the old.

To the right is Passage Angels, which leads into the mediaeval **Barri Jueu** (Jewish Quarter), still proud owner of some of its original Gothic arches. At the end of Santa Anna are some more Roman remains – the walls of the city's Provincial Forum.

Turn left into La Mercería (Haberdasher's Street), which during the Middle Ages was the market area and which still retains its 14th-century arcades. Come here on Sunday morning when the clock is turned back and the area hosts an antique market.

A little further on are the steps up to mediaeval Tarragona's pride and joy – the Romanesque and Gothic **Cathedral**, built between 1171 and 1331 on Tarragona's highest point, where the Roman's had erected a temple to Jupiter. From the front it is rather disappointing, appearing somewhat cramped, with its front towers severely truncated – as if a great gust of wind has

blown the tops clean away. It is difficult to estimate its size from this angle, but the great Gothic doorway, and above it, one of Europe's largest rose windows, give an indication. It is actually the largest cathedral in Catalonia, a province which takes its religious architecture very seriously.

Follow the arrows to the tourist entrance round to the left and you reach the **cloister**, from where the importance of this great building becomes more apparent. Constructed in the 12th and 13th centuries, the cloister is an attraction in its own right. Similar to those of the great local Cistercian monasteries, it is large (measuring some 46m/150ft down each side), airy, and incorporates a pretty, sunny garden. Notice the sculptural detail of the capitals around the cloister. The most famous is the relief

*The lovely Gothic and Romanesque cloister of the Cathedral in Tarragona is a peaceful and contemplative place.*

known as the **Procession of the Rats**, which depicts the rodents conducting a cat's funeral (ask in the museum if you have any difficulty in locating it).

Built into the west gallery is another unexpected feature – a Moslem monument of marble. The date of this *mihrab*, or shrine, is AD 960, and it is thought to have arrived here as a battle trophy.

The cathedral's **Museu Diocesà** boasts a fine collection of ecclesiastical art and ancient objects, including many impressive Flemish tapestries. These are all well-lit and displayed in several rooms round the cloister. The museum also hosts some very high-quality temporary exhibitions.

The overall effect, looking up to the vaulted ceiling inside, is one of austere majesty. This is regarded as one of the finest cathedrals of this period throughout all of Spain. The **main altarpiece**, carved in alabaster by the 15th-century Catalan master, Pere Johan, shows excellent lifelike detail. It is dedicated to Santa Tecla, the local patron saint, who is said to have been converted to Christianity by St Paul, who actually preached in Tarragona. To the right of the altar, look out for the sculpted tomb of Prince Juan de Aragón, an

*Around the cathedral in the mediaeval part of town are many characterful, old-fashioned shops.*

archbishop of the city who died in 1334.

In total there are 19 chapels in the church, ranging in style from high mediaeval art to 19th-century kitsch. The best are those dedicated to: *Nostra Senyora de Montserrat* of the 15th century; *Santa Maria dels Sastres* (of the tailors) of the 14th century; and *Santa Tecla* of the 18th century.

The narrow, cobbled streets surrounding the cathedral have hardly changed since the Middle Ages either. Tiny houses in picturesque decay, shops selling tins and packets usually found in museums of yesteryear, and cross-legged artisans fashioning brooms and wickerwork artefacts using time-honoured ways – all recall a bygone era.

It's worth walking all the way around the cathedral to view it from different angles. Just before you return to the front square, you will see the **Antic Hospital** (Old Hospital) which was constructed between the 12th and 14th centuries and is now a local government office.

Descend the steps from the cathedral square and about a hundred yards to your left, along Carrer Major, is Carrer de la Nau, known for its antique shops. To the right is Vía Cavallers and the **Casa Museu Castellarnau**. The Castellarnaus were a noble, city-dwelling family whose 18th-19th-century mansion has recently been renovated with sumptuous period fittings and a small museum.

## Modern Tarragona and the Port

Tarragona is capital of the 9,842sq km (3,800sq mile) province of the same name, and with a population of over 100,000, is a big town in most respects. Surprisingly, in view of its historical legacy and the number of good beaches literally on its doorstep, it is only just beginning to wake up to the potential of tourism.

The current tourist infrastructure is somewhat limited, and with only five modestly sized hotels with three stars or above, there is a definite **49**

shortage of the mid-to-upper price accommodation. If you want to spend more than a day here, thoroughly recommended to be able to see all the sights, it may be best to stay overnight in Salou (see p.53) or Cambrils (see p.55). The hub of most night-time activity **50** is the Rambla Nova, though the Plaça de la Font can also be quite lively during summer.

Stroll along the **Rambla Nova** to feel the pulse of the city. It's not the same as the bustling Rambla of Barcelona, but it does have the confident air of a city endowed with a rich past and a prosperous present. While walking along the

Rambla, note the Modernist flourishes on buildings. Past the statue of Admiral Roger de Lauria, a swashbuckling 13th-century hero, is the clifftop viewing point known as the **Balcó del Mediterrani** (Balcony of the Mediterranean).

Down to the left is the long, golden strip of the **Platja del Miracle**. It appears scarcely developed, though in summer refreshments and sailing tuition are offered. Follow the coast road east and you'll find more pretty coves and beaches. Watersports tuition is available at Platja Llarga and hire equipment at Platja de la Savinosa, Platja de la Móra, and Platja de l'Arrabassada. The last is probably the best beach, but at most times of year all offer excellent possibilities for **51** delightful uncrowded swimming and sunbathing.

From the Balcó del Mediterrani you can also see the **port** of Tarragona. This is one of the three largest commercial ports in Spain, and one of the busiest in the whole Mediterranean. While the commercial port is not a tourist attraction, the adjacent fishing port is certainly worth a visit. Its waterfront district is unaccountably known as **El Serrall**, meaning 'the harem', but the only conspicuous wives are those sitting on wicker chairs mending voluminous, red fishing nets sprawled out along the quay.

Away from the boats, the harbour and old backstreets of El Serrall are also worth exploring for the area's fish restaurants. Some of Tarragona's finest seafood is served here, often in plain surroundings.

A more up-market venue is the **Club Nàutic**, the oldest sailing club in Catalonia. Have a drink on the balcony and watch the fishing boats and pleasure craft bobbing side by side. They also offer fine food **52** here (see p.78).

# Tarragona to the Ebro Delta

While the coast to the east of Tarragona offers good beaches, historical monuments and several attractive settlements, the strip immediately to the west is given over almost entirely to industry. The petrochemical and oil fumes can get quite strong here.

The first resort, **Pineda de Mar**, is an overspill from

---

### The Salou Armada

Although Salou is not famous for its historical associations, its Llevant beach was in fact the embarcation point for the Armada of King Jaume I in 1229.

His forces successfully wrested Majorca from the Moors, thus adding another territory to the kingdom of Catalonia and earning the king the nickname *El Conquistador* (Conqueror). He is commemorated by a large, modern monument on the promenade which also bears his name.

Salou and offers a fine 3km (2-mile) beach with most facilities. Pineda is particularly popular with young people, mostly due to the waterpark, Acquapark, and the adjacent fashionable nightspot.

**Salou** has been a major cosmopolitan resort for over 20 years, and in many ways is to the Costa Dorada what Benidorm is to the Costa Blanca – a well-ordered, no-frills playground for holidaymakers

on a budget. Its long, sandy beaches, stretching for over 1.5km (1 mile), even bear the same names as those in Benidorm: Llevant/Levante ('sunrise') to the east and Ponente/Poniente ('sunset') to the west.

Llevant, the livelier of the two, is bordered by a palm-shaded promenade dotted with benches and colourful flower arrangements. The east end of the beach is particularly geared to entertainment. Street

stalls sell tourist souvenirs, cafés serve traditional tea, and restaurants dish out German, Dutch and British food, while bars compete to offer the highest number of satellite-television channels. There's even a MacDonalds half-way along the promenade. In the early evening, the crowds gather to watch the town's famous **illuminated fountain**. It was designed by Buigas (famous for his dancing fountains in Barcelona) and has become a symbol of Salou.

Just to the east of Platja Llevant is the relatively small, 200m (650ft) cove of **Platja de Capellans**. Pine trees and tall cliffs help to make this a genuinely attractive spot, but it can get very crowded.

The far end, east of Llevant beach, offers Salou's permanent funfair, good shopping, and a few up-market hotels. At the corner of the promenade and Carrer Barcelona, look out for the Casa Bonet, a beautiful, Modernist mansion designed in 1918-19 by the renowned architect Domènec Sugranyes, who took over the work on Gaudí's unfinished Sagrada Família cathedral in Barcelona (see p.27).

Just inland from the front (behind the railway station) is the town's only major historical structure. The very solid

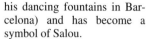

*U*ntangling prawns from the nets at L'Ametlla de Mar means langostinos on the menu.

## Birdwatching in the Ebro Delta

The Ebro Delta is both a major breeding ground for waterfowl, waders and seabirds, and an important resting site for winter migrants. The total bird population stands between 50,000 and 100,000, and includes 60 percent of all species found in Europe. The most common types are from the duck and coot families, though you will also see little egrets and, if you're lucky, flamingos.

The best sites for birdwatching are the more remote parts of the reserve. These include: Punta de la Banya (on the Peninsula dels Alfacs, a breeding ground for flamingos); Punta del Fangar; Ile de Buda (reached by boat); and La Tancada and Salines salt lagoons (which attract flamingos). Dawn and dusk are the best times of day, while the best time of year is October or November, following the rice harvest. Call at the tourist office at Deltebre for the latest information.

**Torre Vella** (Old Tower) was built during the 16th century as a form of protection against Algerian and Turkish pirates. It now houses a museum of modern art.

Platja Ponent also has a pleasant promenade and is a long and busy beach (though alongside Llevant it can seem quite quiet). This merges into the residential suburb of Vilafortuny which in turn drifts into Cambrils. Before you get to Cambrils proper, however, there are some fine pine-shaded beaches on which to relax.

**Cambrils** is an attractive fishing port turned resort. It has a long seafront, and much of its charm stems from the large fleet of *bous* – small fishing boats which carry oversized lamps for night duty – at anchor here. The reliable catch has helped turn Cambrils into a Catalan gourmet town. Its waterfront boasts more good **restaurants** than many a metropolis (almost twice as many  **55**

as Tarragona) and attracts connoisseurs of good food from all over the region.

**Pleasure boats** run regularly between Salou and Cambrils, and also up and down the coast from Cambrils on excursions to L'Ametlla de Mar and Tarragona, as well as to the Sunday market at L'Hospitalet de l'Infant.

Set back from the waterfront at Cambrils is a small, characterful and bustling centre with old, unspoiled streets and a fine indoor market. On the main road, heading south out of town, look out for the fine, old **Torre de l'Ermita** (Tower of the Hermitage), which is next door to the hermitage/church of Mare de Déu del Camí. The tower houses a small museum.

Cambrils is the last major resort on the Costa Dorada. West of here, the coast becomes mostly quiet and undeveloped. There are several minor resorts, however, the first of which is the pleasant beach of **Miami Platja**. (Don't let your judgment be coloured by the name; it's nothing like its Florida namesake.)

Just next door, **L'Hospitalet de l'Infant** (the Hospice of the Prince) is also a small beach resort occupying an attractive setting in a large bay backed by hills. Its name is derived from a 14th-century hospice for pilgrims, whose ruins still remain today.

*The Ebro Delta; a quiet, golden place of rice fields far from the madding crowds.*

A little further along the coast, past the startling red and white nuclear power station of Vandellós, lies **L'Ametlla de Mar**, a quiet, very 'low-tech' fishing village which is well worth a visit. Watch the boats coming in with the catch, or the fishermen and their wives unravelling twisted nets on the quay, disentangling tiny *langostinos* (prawns) and holding them up for your approval. With four beaches close by, L'Ametlla has also become something of a tourist centre.

Just past the small port of **L'Ampolla**, the coastline changes dramatically. Out go the hills and beaches and in their place come great, flat tracts. In spring they're water-logged and give off a blue-green colour; in summer they turn gold when filled with ears of rice, or green with vegetable crops; and in winter they return to bare brown earth.

This is the **Ebro Delta**, the largest wetlands in Catalonia and, after France's famous Carmague, the most important aquatic environment in the

**57**

western Mediterranean. The Delta was created from mud washed down the River Ebro all the way from Zaragoza. The river continues to throw up new land and the Delta expands some 10m (33ft) into the sea each year. It now covers an area of more than 320sq km (123sq miles), of which 7,690ha (19,000 acres), or just under 25 percent of the total area, have been set aside as a protected Natural Park.

The Ebro Delta is a rich agricultural district famous for its rice, though many other fruit and vegetable crops also flourish in the rich soil.

There aren't many roads in this quiet part of the world, but it's still quite possible to get lost, so take care. Follow the road to **Deltebre** (formerly named La Cava) where there is a tourist office. In addition to supplying general information and maps, the office will also be able to advise you on the best places for **birdwatching** (see p.55). Enquire about boat excursions which leave from Deltebre (or you can also **58** hire a boat from Amposta).

You'll need the best part of a day, perhaps more, to explore both north and south of the Delta. If time is limited, stick to the south. Take the old-fashioned *transbordador* (car-ferry, the only way across the Ebro) at Sant Jaume d'Enveja, and head south to the long and rather desolate ocean-like beaches of Platja dels Eucaliptus and Platja del Trabucador. Due south, the Peninsula dels Alfacs is part of the Natural Park, and is off limits to cars.

Unless you are an ornithologist, the principal beauty of the Ebro is its peace, calm, and wide-open space. Like Florida's Everglades, there is no spectacular scenery here (and certainly no alligators!), but there are vignettes of a slower, almost vanished way of life: small, thatched, whitewashed houses; ramshackle smallholders' huts; rice workers sowing and reaping by hand, and villagers cycling languorously between the paddies. Look out too for horses drawing plough-like contraptions which winnow the chaff from the grain on concrete aprons.

When visiting the Delta in spring, summer or early autumn, you should bring mosquito repellent with you .

**Sant Carles de la Ràpita**, with a population of 10,000, is the main town of the Delta, though it is totally unlike any of the tiny agricultural settlements here. Its large, natural harbour serves a prosperous fishing fleet and ship-building industry. What really distinguishes the town, however, is its gigantic main square. It is so enormous for such a small town that there aren't enough public buildings, shops and offices to fill its perimeter (many of the buildings are private houses). It was the brainstorm of Charles III, who envisaged Sant Carles as a port of great significance. The project died with him in 1788, but the great melancholy square remains.

South of Sant Carles is the River Alcanar and the border with the Costa del Azahar. Turn north instead towards Amposta and Tortosa.

**Amposta**, a town of nearly 15,000 on the banks of the Ebro, is a key centre for sports fishing. It's a good place for a coffee stop and there's also a museum about the Delta.

**Tortosa** held a key strategic role for many centuries as the last major town before the sea,

---

### Battle of the Ebro

Due to its strategically important location, the town of Tortosa has witnessed much bloodshed in the course of its long history, but no carnage so terrible as the Battle of the Ebro in 1938. This was one of the worst conflicts of the Spanish Civil War, resulting in an overwhelming victory for Franco's Nationalists, and the loss of as many as 150,000 Republican lives (estimates of casualties vary enormously). A monument to those who fell, in the form of a striking, modern structure, rises arrow-like from a concrete island in the middle of the Ebro.

guarding the Ebro River which runs far into the Spanish interior. The elaborate fortress at the top of the town was built by the Moors, who held out at length here during the 1148 Reconquest. Under the Aragonese kings, it became a royal residence known as the Castle of San Juan. Today it's better known by its Arabic name, **La Zuda** (or Suda), and houses a *parador*. It's a long and steep walk up, so if you would prefer to drive, follow the river a little way out of town and then backtrack up the hill. It's well worth the climb, as this is the only vantage point from where you can take in the whole city, and particularly the cathedral.

From the ground, the **cathedral** is tightly hemmed in, but viewed from on high, it is a splendid sight. Built between the 14th and 16th centuries, it's a fine example of Catalan Gothic architecture. Try not to miss the 14th-century triptych or the 15th-century carved stone pulpits.

From La Zuda, it is also easy to see the remains of the **60** old **city walls**.

# Inland Excursions

## Montserrat

(Tarragona 96km/60 miles)
For 700 years, pilgrims have been climbing the mighty rock formation to reach the **Monastery of Montserrat**. Now that donkeys and foot power have been replaced by cable-cars and coaches, about 1 million people every year make the trip to the spiritual heart of Catalonia.

There have been hermitages here since mediaeval times, possibly to escape the Moorish invasion. One such hermitage was enlarged to become a Benedictine monastery, and in the 12th century it became the repository of a small, brown statue of the Virgin Mary, **La Moreneta** (the Little Dark Madonna). According to legend, this statue was made by St Luke and brought to Barcelona by St Peter. La Moreneta was subsequently adopted as the patron saint of Catalonia, and pilgrims, from commoners to kings, have come to worship her ever since.

*The Monastery of Montserrat is not only a religious shrine, it's a heavenly place for naturalists.*

The original monastery was destroyed in 1808 by Napoleon's troops, and the present one dates from 1874. This is very much a living, working monastery and public entrance is only permitted to the basilica. A highlight of the visit is the famous **Escolania choir**, which sings angelically at 1pm every single day.

The monastery also houses a good **museum**, with works of art by such masters as El Greco, Picasso and Caravaggio, and a fine collection of modern Catalan paintings and archaeological treasures from the biblical Orient, including **61**

**Heavenly Walks**

If you want to escape the crowds at Montserrat, this pristine area is a protected Natural Park and a walker's paradise. There are four main walks, all well signposted. One of these, Santa Cova (30 minutes), leads to the holy cave where *La Moreneta* was supposedly discovered. The other three lead to hermitages: Sant Joan (15-20 minutes from the top of the funicular terminal); Sant Miquel (30 minutes); and Sant Jeroni (1 hour 30 minutes). The views on all the walks are spectacular.

Funiculars climb up the steep hillsides to the start of the walks to Sant Joan and Santa Cova. Although rather expensive, they are well worth the money in terms of breath saved.

Egyptian mummies. Look out for the beautiful, Gothic cloistered section next door.

Complaints are frequently voiced about the commercialization of the grounds of the monastery, and souvenir stalls do proliferate alongside restaurants and a hotel. But even if the aesthetics of such development may be questionable, the monastery's magnificent setting in beautiful protected **mountain parkland** provides inspiration to the most wooden of hearts.

There's really only one way to arrive here and that's by **62 cable-car**. The terminal is on the C1411 Barcelona–Manresa road. Join the queue, then it's up and away, over 1,000m (3,300ft) to the mountain top, probably breaking through the clouds *en route*. The **view** of the mountains, which certainly live up to their name (*montserrat* means 'serrated-' or 'saw-toothed mountain') is magical.

## Poblet

(Tarragona 45km/28 miles)
When you've seen one monastery, you have definitely not seen them all. **Poblet**'s mediaeval fortress-monastery contrasts sharply with Montserrat.

For a start, Poblet usually seems to be less crowded, even though it is the largest and best preserved Cistercian monastery in Europe. While Montserrat clings to its granite eyrie, Poblet sprawls across a green open plateau amid fertile hillsides; and while both have in times past been ruthlessly plundered, Montserrat today is only a structural replica of its true former glory, whereas Poblet is as close to its original mediaeval state as is possible.

*A grey and pink bastion on the green hillside, Poblet is more like a fortress than a monastery.*

Poblet was founded in 1151 by the Count of Barcelona, Ramón Berenguer IV, as a gesture of thanks for the reconquest of Catalonia from the Moors. Continuous royal patronage brought the monastery fame and fortune, as well as historical importance. **63**

The ultimate accolade of royal pantheon (burial place) was bestowed by Peter the Ceremonious during the 14th century. He and seven other kings of Aragon are interred here in unique **tombs** which are suspended on low arches in the cross vault of the church. Only fragments of the original tomb sculptures have been preserved, so the carvings you see today are skilled reproductions.

As you enter the grounds, the **front** of the monastery is a majestic sight. Its towers, belfries, lanterns and walls are as imposing as those of any castle. Poblet is still a working monastery, however, so visitors are not allowed to wander at will. A guided tour takes you past the vaulted wine cellars, the library, chapter-house, the refectory and into the impressive Gothic-Romanesque church. It's big and airy, and in accordance with the Cistercian way of life, shuns any kind of ornamentation.

However, perhaps the real appreciation of the monastic mood comes in the form of the **cloister**. This too is large and atmospheric, with four brooding poplars and a rose garden. Only the trickle of water and bird-song disturbs the serenity. At one time around 200 monks lived and worked here; today there are around 30.

### Andorra

Tour operators all along the Costa Dorada offer gruelling day trips to Andorra, the famous 487sq km (188sq mile) principality huddled between mountain peaks in the Pyrénées. Although it lies in beautiful, unspoilt countryside, most operators simply head for the hypermarkets, since Andorra is free of the taxes which apply to neighbouring France and Spain. Many goods are offered at lower prices, but beware that not all are reduced (check with your courier if you have specific bargains in mind).

# A Selection of Hotels and Restaurants on the Costa Dorada

# Recommended Hotels

Below is a selection of accommodation in different price bands for popular resorts and towns on the Costa Dorada. Book hotels well in advance, particularly if visiting in high season or during a fiesta period. The star rating in brackets after each entry refers to the official government grading system (see ACCOMMODATION on p.116). As a basic guide to room prices, we have used the following symbols (for a double room with bath/shower in high season):

| | |
|---|---|
| I | below 7,000 ptas |
| II | 7,000-14,000 ptas |
| III | 15,000-20,000 ptas |
| IIII | above 20,000 ptas |

Do be aware, however, that out of high season, room rates usually fall sharply.

## BARCELONA

### Hotel Colón    III–IIII
### (4 stars)
*Avenida Catedral, 7*
*Tel. 301 14 00*
*Fax 317 29 15*
This charming town house boasts an unbeatable location opposite the cathedral and was one of Miró's favourite haunts. Ask for one of the two front rooms overlooking the cathedral plaza, where *sardanas* are danced every Sunday. Parking. 151 rooms.

### Hotel España    II
### (2 stars)
*Sant Pau, 9-11*
*Tel. 318 17 58*
*Fax 317 11 34*
An architectural gem, the España is a must if you are looking for atmosphere. Even if the hotel is full, come here for a meal in their splendid Modernist restaurant. 84 rooms.

### Hotel Gotico    II
### (3 stars)
*Jaume I, 14*
*Tel. 315 22 11*
*Fax 315 38 19*
An attractive hotel, well placed in the heart of the Barri Gòtic. The rooms are simple, but tastefully decorated in rustic style. Parking. 70 rooms.

## Hotel Gran Vía  ⏹⏹
(3 stars)
*Gran Vía de les Corts
Catalanes, 642
Tel. 318 19 00
Fax 318 99 97*
This delightful, 19th-century town house is full of old-world charm. The public rooms are richly furnished and decorated throughout with art nouveau fittings. Wheelchair access. 48 rooms.

## Hotel Gravina  ⏹⏹–⏹⏹⏹
(3 stars)
*Gravina, 12
Tel. 301 68 68
Fax 317 28 38*
Conveniently situated near Plaça Catalunya, the Gravina's classical façade conceals a very modern interior. The rooms are on the small side but spotlessly clean. Wheelchair access, parking. 80 rooms.

## Hotel Oriente  ⏹⏹–⏹⏹⏹
(3 stars)
*La Rambla, 45-47
Tel. 302 25 58
Fax 412 38 19*
Barcelona's most venerable hotel still preserves its former glamour and style. The ballroom incorporates part of an old Franciscan monastery, and there is also a wonderful Modernist restaurant.

The rooms tend towards the ordinary, but are large, clean and comfortable. 142 rooms.

## Hotel San Agustín  ⏹⏹
(2 stars)
*Plaça Sant Agustí, 3
Tel. 318 16 58
Fax 317 29 28*
This appealing hotel was converted from a convent about a century ago, and despite its recent refurbishment has lost nothing of its charm. 70 rooms.

## Hotel Suizo  ⏹⏹–⏹⏹⏹
(3 stars)
*Plaça de l'Angel, 12
Tel. 315 41 11
Fax 315 38 19*
Just off Vía Laietana, on the edge of the Barri Gòtic, the Suizo enjoys a prime location. Its recently renovated rooms, each with its own balcony, are spacious, bright and cheerful. 48 rooms.

# SITGES

## Galeon Hotel  ⏹⏹
(3 stars)
*Calle San Francisco, 44-46
Sitges
Tel. (summer) 894 06 12,
(winter) 894 06 60*
Small, friendly and slightly old- **67**

fashioned hotel, nestling in the narrow back streets of the town centre. Private, enclosed garden with a palm-shaded swimming pool. 84 rooms.

## Hotel Antemare ▯▯▯
### (4 stars)
*Verge de Montserrat, 48-50*
*Sitges*
*Tel. 894 70 00*
*Fax 894 63 01*
Six apartment-like buildings make up the elegant Hotel Antemare, established for over 60 years in the heart of the town's quiet residential district. Two swimming pools and extensive fitness facilities are available. Wheelchair access. 112 rooms.

## Hotel Calipolis ▯▯▯
### (4 stars)
*Passeig Marítim*
*Sitges*
*Tel. 894 15 00*
*Fax 894 07 64*
This elegant, modern 11-storey hotel overlooks the main beach and provides every comfort in its well-appointed, spacious rooms. Attractive open-air terraces lead out to the promenade. 157 rooms.

## Hotel Platjador ▯▯▯
### (3 stars)
*Passeig de la Ribera, 35-36*

*Sitges*
*Tel. (summer) 894 50 54,*
*(winter) 894 04 60*
*Fax 894 63 35*
Recommended for its beach-side location, its first-floor swimming pool, and the splendid views from its fifth-floor bar and lounge. 40 very comfortable rooms.

## Hotel Romàntic ▯▯
### (2 star *pension*)
*Sant Isidre, 33*
*Sitges*
*Tel. 894 83 75*
*Fax 894 81 67*
Three 19th-century villas have been combined to form a gem of a hotel in the quiet back streets of Sitges. Tiles, sculptures, wicker, and greenery blend *Modernisme* architecture (see p.14) with old Cuba in the public areas and a delightful garden and bar. All the rooms are traditionally furnished. Very popular with the gay community. 55 rooms.

## Hotel San ▯▯▯–▯▯▯▯
## Sebastián Playa
### (4 stars)
*Port Alegre, 53*
*Sitges*
*Tel. 894 86 76*
*Fax 894 04 30*
A small, attractive, and very well-equipped hotel, overlooking the

quieter beach in Sitges. It's tastefully decorated throughout with smart and simple rooms. There's also a small swimming pool, a terrace, and a good restaurant. 51 rooms.

## Hotel La Santa Maria   ▯–▯▯
### (3 stars)
*Passeig de la Ribera, 52*
*Sitges*
*Tel. 894 09 99*
*Fax 894 78 71*
On the seafront, in the busiest part of town, the Santa Maria is an attractive blend of old and new. It offers recently renovated and attractive rooms, traditionally-furnished lounges and an excellent restaurant. Helpful, friendly owners. 35 rooms. (See also RECOMMENDED RESTAURANTS on p.76).

## Hotel Subur   ▯▯
### (3 stars)
*Passeig de la Ribera*
*Sitges*
*Tel. 894 00 66*
*Fax 894 69 86*
Next door to the Santa Maria, this is a comfortable, unpretentious hotel with air-conditioned rooms and friendly, helpful staff. Ask for a room at the back to escape the road noise. Good restaurant. 95 rooms.

## Hotel Subur Marítim   ▯▯▯▯
### (4 stars)
*Passeig Marítim*
*Sitges*
*Tel. 894 15 50*
*Fax 894 69 86*
An attractive, small, modern hotel with a spacious garden and swimming pool, recently refurbished to a high standard. Located in the quiet residential part of Sitges, the hotel is also close to the beach. 42 rooms.

## Hotel El Xalet   ▯▯
### (no classification)
*Isla de Cuba, 35*
*Sitges*
*Tel. 811 00 70*
A gorgeous, late 19th-century Modernist building which contrasts High Gothic with art nouveau. Lovely swimming pool and garden, and a charming period dining room. Rooms have antique furniture and all mod cons, including air-conditioning. 10 rooms only.

## Sitges Park Hotel   ▯▯
### (3 stars)
*Calle Jesús, 16*
*Sitges*
*Tel. 894 02 50*
*Fax 894 08 39*
Behind the street entrance of this very central hotel is a fairy-tale **69**

Gothic tower which is part of the original building, plus a beautiful palm-shaded terrace and swimming pool. Rooms are fairly basic. 87 rooms.

## ALTAFULLA

### Hotel Faristol    ▌
### (no classification)
*Calle San Martin, 5*
*Altafulla*
*Tel. 65 00 77*
A delightful, 18th-century mansion, typical of old Altafulla, hosted by Señor Marti and his English wife, who treat visitors as house guests. Beautiful period-style decor and plenty of antiques everywhere. Highly recommended. 5 rooms.

## TARRAGONA

### Hotel Astari    ▌–▐▌
### (3 stars)
*Vía Augusta, 95*
*Tarragona*
*Tel. 23 69 11*
A comfortable hotel which is efficiently managed by an Anglophile owner. Pleasant swimming pool and terrace bar with sea views as well as outdoor dining. 83 rooms.

### Hotel España    ▐▐▐▐
### (1 star)
*Rambla Nova, 40*
*Tarragona*
*Tel. 23 27 12*
The Hotel España occupies a tall, narrow, 19th-century building on the busy Rambla. It is quite comfortable, though with few facilities, and is only worth considering out of high season. No restaurant. 40 rooms.

### Hotel Imperial    ▐▐▐▐▐
### Tarraco
### (4 stars)
*Passeig de les Palmeres*
*Tarragona*
*Tel. 23 30 40*
*Fax 21 65 66*
The biggest, best and only 4-star hotel in town, the Imperial is more used to businessmen than tourists, but its good facilities and cliff-top location are perfect for a short or long stay. Swimming pool, tennis court. 170 rooms.

### Hotel Lauria    ▐▐▐▐▐
### (3 stars)
*Rambla Nova, 20*
*Tarragona*
*Tel. 23 67 12*
*Fax 23 67 00*
This very comfortable and modern hotel lies behind the elegant 19th-century Rambla Nova façade. Its

good position means it is only a few yards from the delightful Balcó del Mediterrani (see p.51). No restaurant. 72 rooms.

### Hotel Marina
**(1 star)**
*Vía Augusta, 151*
*Tarragona*
*Tel. 23 30 27*
*Fax 23 33 09*
This small, modern establishment with a leafy front garden, resembles a private house more than a hotel. Modest, clean rooms plus a terrace and tennis court. Conveniently placed for the Platja de l'Arabassada (see p.51). 26 rooms.

### Hotel Nuria
**(2 stars)**
*Vía Augusta, 217*
*Tarragona*
*Tel. 23 50 11*
*Fax 23 50 07*
Modern, unpretentious hotel with restaurant and bar, rooms recently upgraded. Handy for the Platja de l'Arabassada (see p.51). Good value out of season. 61 rooms.

### Hotel Paris
**(3 stars)**
*Maragall, 4*
*Tarragona*
*Tel. 23 60 12*
*Fax 23 86 54*
The front of the Hotel Paris is rather uninspiring, but its rooms have just been renovated and upgraded. It is reasonable value out of high season. Good location just off Rambla Vella. No restaurant. 45 rooms.

### Hotel Sant Jordi
**(2 stars)**
*Vía Augusta*
*Tarragona*
*Tel. 20 75 15*
Roughly 2 km (1½ miles) out of town, the interior of the Hotel Sant Jordi is rather dated, though some rooms do have charming sea views. No restaurant. 40 rooms.

### Hotel Urbis
**(3 stars)**
*Reding, 20*
*Tarragona*
*Tel. 24 01 16*
*Fax 24 36 54*
A member of the Best Western Hotel chain, the centrally located Urbis provides a good international standard of comfort. Very expensive in high season. No restaurant. 44 rooms.

### Pension La Noria
**(2 stars)**
*Plaça de la Font, 53*
*Tarragona*
*Tel. 23 87 17*

If you want to stay centrally on a tight budget, these are quite possibly the best of the cheap rooms in this popular backpacker's area. 24 rooms.

## SALOU

### Hotel Planas
### (2 stars)
*Plaza Bonet, 3*
*Salou*
*Tel. 38 01 08*
The Planas is modern and comfortable (though with modest public areas), and despite being in the centre of town, retains a quiet atmosphere. Meals are served on the attractive tree-shaded terrace. 100 rooms.

### Salou Princess Hotel
### (3 stars)
*Avenida de Andorra*
*Salou*
*Tel. 38 34 12*
*Fax 31 47 64*
Located on the town's quieter stretch of beach, but still close to the centre, the Princess is one of Salou's most elegant hotels. Well-equipped rooms and attractive sun terraces as well as swimming pools draw a cosmopolitan crowd. Wheelchair access. 288 rooms.

## CAMBRILS

### Cambrils Princess
### Hotel
### (3 stars)
*Carretera de Salou a Cambrils*
*Tel. 36 42 83*
*Fax 36 53 51*
This smart hotel, one of the Princess chain, is set in a relatively quiet location on the main road, 2 km (1½ miles) from both Salou and Cambrils, and only a few yards from the beach. Attractive swimming pool, plus sun terraces, tennis court, and crazy golf. Popular with tour operators. Wheelchair access. 400 rooms.

### Hotel Centurion Playa
### (3 stars)
*Carretera de Salou a Cambrils*
*Tel. 36 14 50*
*Fax 36 15 00*
Smart, modern beachside hotel, surrounded by pines, set halfway between Salou and Cambrils. Comfortable, attractive rooms. Swimming pool and sun terrace, good restaurant. 211 rooms.

### Hotel Mónica
### (3 stars)
*Galcerán Marquet, 3*
*Cambrils*
*Tel. 36 01 16*
*Fax 79 36 78*

A comfortable, small hotel in the quiet back streets, yet close to the centre. Bright rooms and lawned garden with palm trees and outdoor pool. Squash court, crazy golf. 56 rooms. (Half-board minimum tariff in high season.)

### Hotel Princep
(3 stars)
*Narcis Monturiol,*
*Plaça de l'Església*
*Cambrils*
*Tel. 36 11 27*
*Fax 36 35 32*
Comfortable family-run hotel in the centre of town. Terrace and solarium plus restaurant. 51 rooms.

### Hotel Residencia
Rovira
(3 stars)
*Avenida Diputación, 6*
*Cambrils*
*Tel. 36 09 00*
*Fax 36 09 44*
Don't be put off by the 1960s façade of this hotel. It conceals a modern interior with a smart restaurant. 58 modest rooms.

### Hotel Tropicana
(2 stars)
*Avenida Diputación*
*Cambrils*
*Tel. 36 01 12*
*Fax 26 01 12*

Modest, quiet, comfortable small hotel set on the main road close to the centre of Cambrils and opposite the beach. Attractive lawn with swimming pool. 28 rooms.

### Maritim Aparthotel
(3 stars)
*Carretera de Cambrils a Salou,*
*km 4,700*
*Tel. 38 55 96*
Large beachside apartment blocks, 2 km (1½ miles) from Cambrils, with swimming pools, large sun terraces, tennis courts, sauna and children's playground. Popular with tour operators. Wheelchair access. 277 apartments.

## TORTOSA

### Parador Castillo de
La Zuda
(3 stars)
*Tortosa*
*Tel. 44 44 50*
*Fax 44 44 58*
*(bookings can be made via Keytel in the UK; tel. 071 402 8182)*
A beautifully-restored mediaeval castle in a majestic position overlooking the town, cathedral and Ebro Valley. Public areas are a bit gloomy, but the rooms are comfortable and in local rustic style. Swimming pool. 82 rooms.

**73**

# Recommended Restaurants

We appreciated the food and service in the restaurants listed below. If you find other places that you think are worth recommending, we would be pleased to hear from you. To give you an idea of the price for a three-course meal per person, without wine, we have used the following symbols:

| | |
|---|---|
| I | under 2,500 ptas |
| II | 2,500-3,500 ptas |
| III | 3,500-4,500 ptas |
| IIII | over 4,500 ptas |

It's advisable to book in advance for dinner at all establishments during high season. Book also for lunch in Barcelona restaurants. (The recommended Barcelona restaurants below are all centrally located.)

## BARCELONA

### Agut                     II
*Gignas, 16*
*Tel. 315 17 09*
Top quality Catalan cuisine in an intimate setting which harks back to the 1930s. Excellent *menu del día*. Very popular, with queues forming and staff eager to hurry you along.

### Amaya                    III
*Rambla Santa Mònica, 20-24*
*Tel. 302 61 38*
Some of the best Basque cooking in the city can be found at this friendly establishment. Particularly good on Sunday. Look out for *cocochas a las vasca* (Basque bar-

bels) and *chipirones del norte* (baby squid).

### Can Majo              III–IIII
*Almirall Aixada, 23*
*Tel. 310 14 55*
An intimate and very popular fish restaurant in a rather seedy part of La Barceloneta. Try the *arroz a banda* or the excellent *paella*. Closed Monday and all August.

### Los Caracoles          II–III
*Escudellers, 14*
*Tel. 302 31 85*
This restaurant *típico* is a minor legend in the Barri Gòtic, and serves classic Catalan cuisine at a reasonable price. It's patronized by opera and theatre personalities,

whose signed photographs decorate the walls.

## La Cuineta    |||–||||

*Carrer Paradis, 4*
*Tel. 315 01 11*
This atmospheric restaurant is set in the 17th-century vaults of a wine cellar right in the heart of the Barri Gòtic. Excellent traditional Catalan cuisine; in particular, the *bacalla* (salt cod) is very popular. Closed Monday.

## Egipte    |–||

*Jerusalem, 3*
*Tel. 317 74 80*
Just behind the Rambla's Bo-quería market, the ever-popular Egipte serves basic, well-prepared Catalan dishes, including huge desserts. Arrive early for a table on the balcony. Closed Sunday. (If you can't get in here, try its young trendy sister restaurant, also called Egipte, near the Liceo at Rambla de les Flors, 79.)

## El Gran Café    |||–||||

*Avinyó, 9*
*Tel. 318 79 86*
A delightful, 1920s-style restaurant on two floors, close to the Rambla, serving French and Catalan food. Pianist in the evenings. Closed Saturday lunch, all day Sunday and all August.

## Les Set Portes    ||

*Passeig de Isabel II, 14*
*Tel. 319 30 33*
A venerable institution, now designated an architectural monument and little changed since it opened in 1836. A reasonably priced, extensive menu of Catalan food served to up to 1,000 diners in any of the restaurant's seven rooms, from 1pm to 1am daily.

# SITGES

## Cap de la Vila    ||

*Cap de la Vila*
*Tel. 894 10 91*
Lively, bright and cheerful Italian pizza parlour at a busy pedestrianized crossroads in the old town. Ideal for a snack or a meal with the children. Friendly staff.

## Casa Hidalgo    |–||

*Carrer Sant Pau, 12*
*Tel. 894 38 95*
A traditional restaurant, serving a good selection of meat and fish dishes, such as Goat *à la Castellana*, or plaice in orange sauce.

## El Greco    ||–|||

*Passeig de la Ribera, 70*
*Tel. 894 29 06*
Local and international dishes served in comfortable surroundings **75**

here, in one of the town's best restaurants. Try *langostinos a Calisay* on the seafront terrace.

### Mare Nostrum ‖
*Passeig de la Ribera, 60*
*Tel. 894 33 93*
Long-established, elegant but informal seafront restaurant, with a pleasant terrace and an attractive nautically-themed dining room. Regional dishes include shrimp *romesco*, hake with *cava*, chicken and crayfish. Closed Wednesday.

### La Masia ‖‖
*Passeig Vilanova, 164-166*
*Tel. 894 10 76*
Splendid, traditional farmhouse setting with garden terrace. Personalities from near and far come for the huge portions of excellent local food.

### Oliver's ‖
*Isla de Cuba, 39*
*Tel. 894 35 16*
Tucked away in a back street, Oliver's serves up interesting Spanish and international dishes. Very experienced and friendly owner-chef and wife team. Smart dining room. Closed Monday.

### Els Quatro Gats ‖
*Carrer Sant Pau, 13*
*Tel. 894 19 15*

Traditional, informal and intimate, the 'Four Cats' pays homage to Picasso's favourite Barcelona restaurant. Good value Spanish and regional dishes, very reasonable *menu del día*.

### La Santa Maria ‖–‖
*Passeig de la Ribera, 52*
*Tel. 894 09 99*
The most popular place in town – the front terrace of this seafront restaurant is always packed. Long menu, efficient service, huge portions, good at all times of the day. Try the *paella* or the *zarzuela*.

### El Velero ‖‖–‖‖‖
*Passeig de la Ribera, 38*
*Tel. 894 20 51*
Fine dining in elegant semi-formal surroundings on the seafront. Excellent fish dishes; start with salmon, elvers and crab, and try the prawns in peach sauce. Closed Sunday night and all day Monday.

## ALTAFULLA

### Hotel Faristol ‖–‖
*Calle San Martin, 5*
*Tel. 65 00 77*
A beautifully-restored Catalan mansion (see RECOMMENDED HOTELS p.70), where meals are served in an atmospheric dining room or

in a lovely walled garden. Specialities include seafood mousse with *cava*. Booking is essential. The restaurant is open weekends only October to July.

## TARRAGONA

### Asador Fernando    ▯–▯▯
*Calle Armanyà, 6*
*No telephone*
Set just off the Rambla Nova, this excellent restaurant and *tapas* bar specializes in Basque cooking with the accent on seafood. Good value *menu del día*.

### Cal Brut    ▯
*Sant Pere, 14, El Serrallo*
*Tel. 24 14 05*
This tiny restaurant is set in a backstreet parallel to the dockside, but dining here is just as good as – and cheaper than – on the front. Fish with *romesco* sauce is the speciality. Closed Sunday afternoon and all day Wednesday.

### Cal Marti    ▯–▯▯
*Sant Pere, 12, El Serrallo*
*Tel. 21 23 84*
Similar in style and atmosphere to its neighbour, Cal Brut, though a little more expensive, Cal Marti is famous for its seafood and authentic fisherman's dishes. Closed Sunday afternoon, all day Monday, and for part of September.

### El Far    ▯
*Rompeolas, Port de Tarragona*
*Tel. 24 41 51*
The 'lighthouse' restaurant is, unsurprisingly, situated on the edge of the water, below the actual lighthouse, with fine sea views. Delicious fish is cooked simply and served without fuss, in a cheery, informal atmosphere.

### Les Fonts de Can Sala    ▯▯
*Carretera de Valls (N240), 62*
*Tel. 22 85 75*
An attractive restaurant decorated in rustic Catalan fashion and with the added delight of a lovely tree-shaded terrace. They specialize in typical Catalan cooking and *cuina de mercat* ('market cuisine'), which makes use of fresh inland produce). Closed Tuesday.

### La Guingueta    ▯▯▯
*Les Coques, 9*
*Tel. 23 15 68*
This comfortable restaurant lies close to the cathedral at the centre of the old town. Come here for Catalan *nouvelle cuisine* and *cuina de mercat* ('market cuisine') using the freshest of inland produce. Closed Sunday and for the first fortnight in August.

**77**

## Mistral

*Plaça de la Font, 19*
*Tel. 23 72 22*
Pizzas and pastas are the Mistral's staples, though of course, you could also splash out on a fish *romesco*. Most people come here to enjoy dining in the open air on the Plaça. Closed Sunday.

## Nàutico

*Explanada del Port, El Serrallo*
*Tel. 24 00 62*
The smartest restaurant in the port and the dining room of Catalonia's oldest sailing club, the Club Nautic (see p.52). Relax with a drink on the balcony overlooking the port before a fish feast. Dining room has panoramic views.

## Pa Amb Tomaca

*Lleida, 8*
*Tel. 24 00 45*
As the name suggests, typical Catalan cuisine is always the order of the day in this comfortable restaurant close to the Roman local Forum. Closed Sunday.

## La Puda

*Moll de Pescadors, 25,*
*El Serrallo*
*Tel. 21 10 70*
A no-frills fisherman's café, with a cheerful area of gingham tablecloths set aside for more formal dining. Try the *entremeses de la casa* for a bit of everything, and look out for the interesting daily specials on offer.

## La Rambla

*Rambla Nova, 10*
*Tel. 23 87 29*
This well-run restaurant enjoys a good location near the Balcó del Mediterrani and specializes in rice and *romesco* dishes. Eat out on the terrace and watch the bustle of the Rambla.

## Sol Ric

*Vía Augusta, 227*
*Tel. 23 68 29*
This excellent, outdoor garden restaurant has been serving what many critics regard as the best food in Tarragona since 1959. Fish and shellfish dominate the menu, with *romesco* specials. Closed Sunday night and all day Monday.

## El Tiberi

*Marti d'Ardenyà, 5*
*Tel. 23 54 03*
Don't be put off by the somewhat drab exterior, inside they serve an excellent help-yourself buffet, prepared by one of the town's best chefs. A good place to sample several traditional Catalan dishes at once. Closed Sunday night and all day Monday.

## Trabadoira ||
*Apodaca, 7*
*Tel. 21 00 27*
A comfortable restaurant, a short walk from the Rambla Nova, with a good reputation for seafood.

## Les Voltes ||
*Trinquet Vell, 12*
*Tel. 21 88 30*
Atmospheric location within the vaults of the old Roman Circus; high-tech fittings meet ancient stone. Spanish and international cuisine. Try the *arròs negre* (black rice). Closed Sunday evening.

## SALOU

## Beim Klaus |
*Calle Rodriguez de Pomatta*
*Tel. 38 35 29*
Small, cheerful bistro tucked away off the main promenade with a varied menu of North European staples, such as Dutch Herring on black bread, smoked pork with *sauerkraut*, and a special, Viking Stroganoff. It's popular with the British. Friendly owners and staff.

## Casa Font ||||
*Calle Colon, 17*
*Tel. 38 04 35*
One of Salou's best and longest-established gourmet restaurants,

with a stylish dining room overlooking the beach. Mediterranean and international cuisine prepared by *el patrón*. Closed Monday.

## La Goleta ||
*Platja des Capellans*
*Tel. 38 35 66*
Elegant restaurant facing onto the beach. Relax on the terrace at lunchtime or dine romantically by night inside. Spanish international cuisine; try the partridge in pickle sauce or the prawns in Madeira.

## CAMBRILS

## Berganti ||
*Consolat del Mar, 6*
*Tel. 79 13 37*
Small and friendly with a pretty terrace, this is a good place to get acquainted with Cambrils' piscean delights at a reasonable price. Several types of *zarzuela*, and good value lobster specials.

## El Caliu ||–||
*Pau Casals, 22*
*Tel. 36 01 08*
This *tipica Catalana* specializes in hearty barbecued meat dishes, served outdoors on the terrace or in the rustic gingham-decorated dining room. There's also a good choice of desserts.

**79**

## Can Bosch  ▯▯▯▯

*Rambla Jaime, 1-19*
*Tel. 36 00 19*
Elegant, very modern fish and seafood restaurant, boasting one *Michelin* rosette. Try the excellent turbot with truffles or the equally delicious sautéd baby octopus with scampi. Closed Sunday night and all day Monday.

## Eugenia  ▯▯▯▯

*Consolat de Mar, 80*
*Tel. 36 01 68*
Enjoy excellent fish and seafood either on the shaded terrace, or inside the elegant, old-world dining room. Eugenia's owner is also the town mayor, and a friendly mine of information on all aspects of Cambrils.

## Joan Gatell-Casa Gatell  ▯▯▯▯

*Passeig Miramar, 26*
*Tel. 36 00 57*
This superb, seafront restaurant, which has been awarded a *Michelin* rosette, is owned and managed by the town's pioneering culinary Gatell family. Fish and seafood par excellence feature; try the *entremeses Gatell*, the *boullabaisse*, or the *arroz marinera*. Ask for a table by the window on the first floor. Closed Sunday night and all day Monday.

## Marina  ▯▯

*Passeig Miramar, 42*
*Tel. 36 04 32*
Attractive family-run seafront restaurant with a lovely terrace looking onto the harbour. Fish and seafood predominate.

## Mas Gallau  ▯▯▯

*Carretera Valencia–Barcelona, 4km/2.5 miles east of Cambrils*
*Tel. 36 05 88*
Superb setting in an atmospheric re-creation of a beamed and stuccoed traditional Catalan *masia* (farmhouse). Extensive Spanish regional menu, try *escudella* followed by rabbit, or pig's trotters with *escargots à la Catalane*.

## Pizzeria Roma  ▯▯

*Plaça Cataluña, 2*
*Tel. 36 10 46*
Pizzas and pastas, plus meaty Italian and North European dishes, make up most of the menu here. The decor is traditional rustic and tables spill out onto the side street.

## Rovira Antiguo  ▯▯

*Passeig Miramar, 37*
*Tel. 36 01 05*
Elegant, traditional restaurant facing onto the promenade, with an attractive enclosed front terrace. Typical regional meat and fish dishes, plus seafood specialities.

## Santes Creus

(Tarragona 36km/22 miles)
About 40km (25 miles) from Poblet, another great **monastery** sprawls among the vineyards. Santes Creus (Holy Crosses), a Cistercian foundation, was established just six years after Poblet, in 1157. Comparisons with Poblet are obvious. Santes Creus is much smaller and less grand, but even from within the shadow of its bigger and more famous neighbour, it is still an architectural masterpiece.

The **cloisters** are once again a highlight (two here). The Great Cloister is classic Catalan Gothic, dating to the 14th century, and includes some uncharacteristically light-hearted touches. Look out for heraldic designs, animals, and humorous faces carved on the arches and walls. The Infirmary cloister is plain and very peaceful.

There is also a superb vaulted **chapter-house** with tombs of 16th-century abbots set into the floor and, upstairs, a spacious **dormitory** with a large timber-arched roof.

Santes Creus was the royal resting place before the honour passed to Poblet, and two kings are buried here. Peter the Great (*Pere II* or *Pedro el Grande* who died in 1285) lies in a splendid **Gothic tabernacle** and close by is the beautifully sculpted tomb of Peter's son, James the Just, who died in 1327. Santes Creus also reveals its regal connections in the remains of the living quarters – the **Royal Palace**, built on the orders of Peter II. These surround a perfect 14th-century patio of delicate arches and a lovely staircase.

The monastery, disbanded in 1835, and then pillaged, was never re-established. Instead, it became a parish church and was recently taken over by the state as a museum.

## Vilafranca del Penedés

(Tarragona 51km/32 miles)
The town of **Vilafranca del Penedés** is situated on a fertile plain, midway between Barcelona and Tarragona. Over the last two centuries, Vilafranca has literally grown its **81**

own success story, helping the Penedés become one of the best-known wine regions.

There are no *bodegas* to visit in the centre of town, but you will find one of Spain's very best wine museums, the **Museu del Vino** – and you don't have to be a connoisseur to appreciate the exhibits. Dioramas illustrate wine through the ages and you can see huge, wooden **wine presses** used to crush grapes when the Romans were in the province. Another hall displays the glass bottles and jugs which have quenched centuries of thirst, and there is even an art gallery devoted to the noble vine.

The wine museum shares its quarters with the **Museu Municipal**, which is devoted to geology, archaeology, natural history, and Catalan religious art. Formerly a mediaeval palace of the counts of Barcelona and the kings of Aragon, the building is an attraction in its own right. Look out from the third-floor windows and you will be able to see a monument to another of Vilafranca del Penedés' passions – a 5-storey

*One of the fine old tombs in Santes Creus (above), and the Freixenet cava cellars (right).*

human pyramid team of *castellers* (see p.92).

But Vilafranca is not just for wine-lovers or balancing acts. Its leafy Rambla and old town are full of character, particularly on Saturday when it hosts one of the region's most colourful general **markets**. Visit the splendid **Basilica of Santa Maria**, the adjacent **Palais Baltà**, and the church of **Sant Francesc**, which is famous for its Catalan Gothic treasures.

Pick up a map from the helpful tourist office in the town hall and ask them about visits to nearby vineyards. The **Torres vineyard**, which lies a short distance out of town, is king of the Catalan labels, and one of the world's great wine producers. Torres is known for its technical innovation and all its wines are made in temperature-controlled stainless steel vats. The tour reflects this, and traditionalists are likely to feel that such methods take the romance out of the vine. If that's the case, you may well find the tours at **Sant Sadurní d'Anoia** (12km/7 miles to the north east) more interesting.

Sant Sadurní is famous as the centre of production of the sparkling *cava* (see p.112), and several **cava houses** are open to visitors. Here you descend to deep cellars where the wine is stored at a constant temperature, and the method of manufacture (identical to that for Champagne) is explained. The tour at **Freixenet** (pronounced fre-JER-nay with a soft 'j' as in the French *je*) is recommended. **Cordoníu** also

puts on a good tour and is renowned for its interesting Modernist buildings.

## Reus and Montblanc

(Tarragona 13km/8 miles and 38km/24 miles)

**Reus** is the place which every charter tourist flies into, yet few return to properly explore; which is a shame, because this is a bustling and characterful provincial centre.

The centre is the **Plaza de España**, an elegant square, porticoed on one side and little changed (traffic aside) since the 19th century. Reus' most famous son was Antoni Gaudí, born here in 1852, but surprisingly he has left no marks of any significance in his hometown. Instead the task was left to his followers. The ornate **Casa de Navàs** on the Plaza de España is the town's finest Modernist building.

For refreshment of body as well as mind seek out the **Café de Reus**, a softly-lit Modernist gem with gleaming brass and etched glass reminiscent of a **84** British Victorian pub. It's just

off Plaza Mercalada which adjoins Plaza de España. You're unlikely to miss the imposing 16th-century church of **Sant Pere**, and there are also two museums: the rated Museu d'Arqueologia Salvador Vilaseca, and the Comarcal, featuring sculpture and architecture.

The town is at its best on a Monday which is **market day**. Nuts and dried fruit gathered from the countryside are local specialities.

**Montblanc** lies 25km (15 miles) north east of Reus and is the capital of its province. There any similarity ends, for this is a compact **walled town**, where many of the monuments date from the 14th century. The tourist office will provide you with a good town plan.

Go to the **Plaça Major** and look in the lobby of the town hall. The building dates from the 13th century, though its present front is 400-500 years

*Market day at Vilafranca del Penedés; colourful produce, colourful characters.*

younger. Opposite the town hall, the building with the balcony is known as the **Casal dels Desclergue**. This is the former residence of a *veguer*, the king's representative in the 16th century, when Montblanc was one of the most important towns in Catalonia. The 13th-century **Palau Reial** (Royal Palace) is just a few yards away, but is much altered from its original state.

The town's major monument is the Gothic church of **Santa Maria la Major** (follow the street opposite Casal dels Desclergue). But it's fun just to wander in Montblanc, spotting vestiges of the ancient past in old buildings, and of the recent past in old-fashioned shop windows.

There are two **museums** in the walled town. The regional museum is in the 18th-century Casal Josa, and the Museu Marés (painting and sculpture) is in the church of Santa Marçal. Two **churches** worth a

look are Sant Miquel and Sant Francesc, both 13th-century, and both home, at different times, to the mediaeval *Corts Catalan* (Catalan parliament).

**Espluga de Francolí**, 10km (6 miles) to the north, is worth a visit for its **Museu de Vidra Rural** (Rural Life Museum). This display of life as it was in the mainly agricultural Conca de Barberà province, covers

four floors of an 18th-century house and is bright and cheery.

## Samá Park and Escornalbou

(Cambrils, 4km/2½ miles and 18km/11 miles)
Note – Samá Park is only open on Sunday.
As you head north from Cambrils on the road to Montbrió

*A mural inside the foyer of the Town Hall at Montblanc illustrates the local history of wine production.*

86

del Camp, there is a very curious sight at the junction with the road to Reus and Vinyols. On top of a small mountain stump, inset with viewing balconies, is a **mediaeval castle tower**. Stranger still, a bride and groom may well wave to you from the tower! Turn right down this road; the entrance to **Samá Park** is on the left.

This fantasy park, begun in 1881, was the brainchild of Don Salvador Samá Torrens, a Cuban heir who wanted to bring some of the atmosphere of the lost Spanish colony to the Costa Dorada. Its walled grounds cover 14ha (35 acres) and contain a lake, waterfalls, ornate fountains, and abundant **exotic flora**, including yuccas, banana and mandarin trees, Indian nettle trees, various palms, and a 20m (66ft) high Mexican species which both grows and lives with its roots in water.

It is a popular place with just about everybody: children tackle the look-out towers, the 'pirate cave', and the play area; newly-weds come here to pose for romantic photographs à deux; and the Cambrils locals enjoy a relaxing Sunday stroll.

Continue east to Montbrió del Camp and Riudecanyes and follow the signs to the **Monestir/Castell d'Escorn albou**. The ancient monastery and castle sit high on top of a hill, which ascends steeply to a height of over 640m (2,100ft).

The monastery was built between the 13th and 15th centuries, but was destroyed in the secular purge of 1835 and much of it is now a romantic ruin. The solid Romanesque **church** has been well restored in recent years, however, and the castle-residence exhibits pottery, furniture and several archaeological finds. A cloister wall has been rebuilt, and today the distant countryside can be seen through its arches.

On a clear, sunny day, the **views** from here are marvellous, and you can enjoy a walk along the old 'monks' path'. On a cool and misty day, however, it's becomes entirely different – a brooding, lonely sort of spot – and few visitors hang around for long after dusk. **87**

# What to Do

## Sport

Long, white, sandy beaches combined with several well-equipped marinas and sailing clubs make the Costa Dorada an obvious watersports destination. Inland the choice is more limited, but the mild climate does confirm the exhortations of the Catalonian tourist board that the sporting season does last indeed *tot l'any* ('all year round').

## Watersports

Equipment and boats are for hire at most of the 22 marinas (*ports esportius*) dotted along the coast. Several beaches, including Platja del Miracle and Platja Llarga (both in Tarragona), Salou, Calafell, Sitges, Cunit, Coma-ruga and Torre-

dembarra, also offer tuition in sailing (catamarans) and wind-surfing. Equipment is also available for hire at several other beaches. Water-skiing is not so widespread – but try Platja Llarga, Salou/LaPineda, and Sitges. You may also find jet-skiing, parasailing, and the water 'sausage' here.

## Fishing

The Ebro Delta is the best place for dangling a line, and Amposta in particular is re-nowned as a sport-fishing cen-tre. You may be able to buy a licence from the tourist office; if not they will direct you to the appropriate licensing and rod-hire outlets.

## Golf

Although golf has been played in Catalonia since 1914, there are, surprisingly, only 16 clubs

*Young fishermen are always hopeful for a bite off the rocks at Sitges.*

in the whole region. Most of these, however, are of a good standard. The main clubs on the Costa Dorada are (from east to west):

*Reial Club de Golf El Prat* (*36 holes*). Not far from Bar-celona Airport, this is the most prestigious club in the region and a regular venue for inter-national competitions. The ter-rain is mostly flat and features pine woods and water hazards. Spectators can also enjoy pad-dle tennis and *pétanque*, or a dip in the swimming pool.

*Terramar* (*18 holes*). Estab-lished at the west end of Sit-ges since 1922, this long, challenging course (5,761m/ 6,302yd) is half coastal, half inland, with narrow fairways and small greens guarded by bunkers and water. The pleas-ant clubhouse includes tennis courts and a swimming pool.

*Costa Daurada* (*9 holes*). A few kilometres north east of Tarragona, this varied course lies amid gently rolling coun-tryside and features bunkers and water hazards. There is also a good clubhouse with squash courts.

**89**

*Reus Aiguësverd* (*18 holes*). Located between Reus and Cambrils, in a delightful setting of olive groves, carob and cypress trees, this gently sloping course is one of the longest in the country (6,314m/6,907yd), with very challenging greens and water hazards, including three lakes and an 'island' hole.

*Bonmont Tres Noves* (*18 holes*). A lovely, spacious Robert Trent Jones course with natural and artificial hazards, near to Montroig del Camp (10km/6 miles north west of Cambrils). The top-class facilities you can enjoy here include swimming pools, squash courts and tennis courts.

There are also golf clubs at L'Ametlla de Mar, Sant Andreu de Llavaneres, and in the Barcelona area. Most clubs are open all year round, and some close on Mondays.

## Horse Riding

The conditions and climate are perfect for this relaxing pastime, but *hípicos* (equestrians) often seem reluctant to advertize to tourists. Enquire at the tourist office for local details.

## Tennis

If there are no courts at your hotel or apartment, it may be possible to arrange the use of courts with a friendly neighbour. Municipal courts will be available in the larger towns and resorts, and some golf clubs also have tennis courts (see above).

## Spectator Sports

Spectator sports are either limited to local events (enquire at a tourist office), or require a trip to Barcelona.

The main spectator sport is **football**, and in particular any matches involving the beloved Futbol Club de Barcelona ('Barça'), whose every kick and tackle is followed and discussed with an almost religious fervour. The marvellous **Camp Nou Stadium** holds 120,000 people, but don't just turn up and expect to get a ticket – you'll have to book well in advance.

# Folklore and Festivals

Catalonia celebrates its festivals just as vigorously as the rest of Spain. Religious and civic holidays seem to be declared at the drop of a hat, so it's likely that you'll encounter at least one in the vicinity during your holiday. Each and every festival is different, but there are also certain practices and rituals that are common to most.

## Sardana

The best-known Catalan folklore expression is the dance known as the *sardana*. To the outsider this seems a sedate, perhaps even dull affair; but to a Catalan patriot it implies

*The sardana is popular with all ages. It's not just a dance, but an affirmation of Catalan solidarity.*

91

an uncommon degree of participation and a literal bonding between people of all ages.

A group joins together in a circle, hold their hands high, and to a musical accompaniment, alternate between slow, thoughtful steps and medium-tempo bouncy kicking. It's not really a spectator event, so once you know roughly what is going on, break into the circle (but not between the man and the lady to his right) and follow the dancers' example. Each *sardana* lasts for around 10 minutes. The band is traditionally an 11-piece ensemble, often made up of crusty-look-ing old gentlemen who might well have been dusted off and brought out just for the occasion. *Sardanas* take place at festivals, parties, family gatherings, or simply because it's the weekend.

## Ball dels Bastons

A more specialist fiesta dance – which you join at your own peril – is the *ball dels bastons* ('dance of the sticks'). Men and boys wearing a kind of Morris-dancer costume beat sturdy, knuckle-bruising sticks together in a hybrid of dancing, fencing and jousting.

---

### Castellers in Spain

The most spectacular of all Catalonia's many folklore celebrations is surely the art of the *castellers*. These are the men and boys who climb barefoot onto one another's shoulders to form human towers which reach up to seven storeys high. The most pampered participant is the young boy who scampers to the very top of the tower and takes the crowd's cheers. The unsung heroes, however, are the *behemoths* at the very bottom of the pile who hold the pyramid up.

  *Castellers* appearances are not that common, so catch them while you can. The team from Valls are acclaimed as being the kings of their art.

*F*iestas are a serious business; discussing tactics for dancing the ball dels bastons!

## Devils and Dragons

A Spanish fiesta is nothing without fireworks and firecrackers, and in Catalonia this is the cue for the entrance of *diables* (devils) and *el drac* (a dragon).

The devils are men and boys dressed in sackcloth costumes with horns and tails. Above their heads they hold special, wooden frames, on which they rotate flaming fireworks as they march through the crowd. If this sounds a little alarming, then look out for the dragon! Pausing only to grab a mouthful of fresh firecrackers and explosive devices, the dragon crew charge through the narrow streets, spewing fire and sparks in all directions and scattering the crowd with excited yelps. It's easy to see in advance what route the dragon will take, since shopkeepers

board their windows in order to prevent firework damage. It's both deafening and great fun, but do protect your eyes and keep small children at a safe distance.

## Gegantes and Capgrosses

Another thoroughly Catalan and colourful fiesta characteristic is the presence of *gegantes* (giants) and *capgrosses* (big heads). The former are towering papier mâché figures **93**

– kings and queens or lords and ladies – measuring up to 4.5m (15ft) high, which are controlled by skilled crews hidden beneath. As they march the streets, they may stop for a 'chat' with spectators leaning out of first-floor windows, before suddenly whirling full circle – much to the amusement (and no doubt consternation) of the crowds beneath them. The *capgrosses* are cartoon-like figures with large,

papier mâché heads, who play the part of jesters complementing the stately *gegantes*.

## Festa Major

Each town and village celebrates the national holidays, but the main festival, literally termed the *festa major*, is held on the local saint's day, which varies between areas. After the *sardanas*, *gegantes*, *diables*, *el drac* and so on, a street dance

is usually held. The larger towns pulsate well into the early hours with South American rhythms, while a no-expense-spared firework display illuminates the sky.

## Harvest Grapes

Autumn brings the harvest festival, and on the Costa Dorada that means grapes. Both Tarragona and Sitges host lively celebrations including teams of young men treading grapes in a competition to see who can make the most 'wine' in a given time. Harvest Queens in traditional costume will be among the crowd watching the frantic footwork.

## Carnaval

*Carnaval* (Carnival), always held the week before Lent, is the other big event of the year and combines the best of Rio- and Catalan-style celebrations. Sitges is very much the place to be during *Carnaval*. Take your camera along to snap some of the amazing costumes worn by both sexes. (Not an occasion for the prudish!)

## Verge Mercè

In late September, Barcelona is the place to be for the week-long *Verge Mercè* (Our Lady of Mercy) celebrations, which

Y ou've never seen such frantic footwork as at the annual grape-treading competition!

**95**

combine traditional festivities with an international festival of theatre, song, dance, and music of all types.

## Other Festivals

The following are a selection of the year's major festivals and some principal venues:

### February/March

Sitges: *Carnaval* (see p.95).

Sitges: International Vintage Car Rally.

### March/April

Montserrat, Poblet: *Setmana Santa* (Holy Week, week preceding Easter). Processions and religious celebrations in all towns.

### April

Barcelona: *Diada de Sant Jordi* (St George's Day, also Cervantes Day). Book fairs, and the Day of Lovers.

### May

Callella: *Festes de Primavera* (Spring Festival). Folk-dancing, vintage cars, bands.

### May/June

Sitges: *Festes del Corpus Christi.* The streets are beautifully carpeted with flowers. Music, dancing and fireworks.

### June

Callella: *Aplec de Sardanas.* Catalonia's most important folkdance festival.

Valls: *Dia de Santa Joan* (24 June). Folklore and *castellers*.

### July

Arenys de Mar: *Festa major.* Celebrations at sea and ashore.

### August

Valls: *Festes del Firagost* (Assumption). Harvest celebrations, folklore, and religious procession.

Vilafranca del Penedés: *Festa major.* Religious procession and *castellers*.

### September

*La Diada* (11 September). Catalonia's national day is celebrated by everyone throughout the region.

Barcelona: *Festes de la Verge Mercè* (around 24 September, see p.95).

Tarragona: *Festa major (de Santa Tecla).* Religious and folklore spectacles, including *castellers*.

### September/October

Sitges, Tarragona: *Festes de la Verema* (grape-harvest festival). Tastings, dancing and competitions (see p.95).

**96**

# The Bullfight

Bullfighting is not a popular Catalan pastime, but if you want to see what it's all about, head for the area's two main *plazas de toros* (bullrings) in Barcelona.

To the Spanish, the bullfight is not regarded as a sport, and even less a contest between two equals. It is simply a ritualistic way of slaughtering a bull. Yet, every time a *torero* (bullfighter) enters the ring, he is in danger, and tragedy does sometimes occur. This is the exception, however, just as an exciting and theatrical bullfight is the exception. In fact, you are far more likely to be bored than repulsed.

The sequence of a bullfight is clearly laid out. First the *matador* gets the measure of the bull with his large red and yellow *capote* (cape), and then the *picadores* (mounted spearmen) arrive. They attempt to lance the bull's neck muscles in order to lower the head and make the *matador*'s kill easier.

Following the *picadores* are the *banderilleros*, on foot, who plant long, coloured darts into the hump on the bull's neck. Finally, the *matador* returns and taunts the bull with the small dark red *muleta* cape. When the *matador* thinks he has achieved domination and the moment is right, he delivers his *coup de grâce* – in theory a single, swift sword stroke over the bull's horns and down between the shoulder blades into the heart. In practice, it often takes more than one attempt.

The season for the *corrida* (bullfight) lasts from March to October.

# Flamenco

Spain's best known entertainment after the bullfight is flamenco – throbbing guitars, stamping heels, and songs that well up from the soul. Many of the songs resemble the wailing chants of Arab music, which may indicate Moorish origins.

Flamenco is very much an Andalusian art form and is therefore quite foreign to Catalonia, but numerous *tablaos* **97**

*Waterparks are guaranteed fun for all – just pluck up courage and take the plunge.*

# For Children

Long, sunny days and soft, sandy beaches mean that the Costa Dorada is a favourite family destination. Off-beach options for older children are limited, but many hotels have special features for the young, ranging from child-minding to supervised poolside games.

On the whole, nightlife for the kids on the Costa Dorada isn't very organized, but there are few, if any, restrictions on children coming out with you to bars and restaurants. Large hotels may also organize children's evening activities.

When the appeal of splashing in sea water and building sandcastles starts to wear thin, try some of the following:

## Make a Splash

Waterparks are usually the favourite activity off the beach. You'll find **Acquapark** (the biggest) at La Pineda (next to Salou). Others include: Aquatic Paradis, just outside Sitges; Marineland, at Malgrat de Mar on the Costa Maresme; and El

(floorshows) are staged in tourist spots and hotels.

There are two main types of flamenco song: the first, bouncy and cheerful, is known as *cante chico*; the other, dark and soulful, is the *cante jondo*, performed in the slow, piercing, melodramatic style of the **98** great flamenco artists.

Acuatico, close to Barcelona. At Acquapark, while the kids hurl themselves down the 'kamikaze' or ride the 'super tobogan', you can sunbathe in the landscaped gardens. Additional park attractions include mini-golf and ten-pin bowling. Marineland also features dolphins, performing parrots and seals, and many more animals.

## Go-karting

Go-kart tracks are common along the coast. The track on the Salou–Reus road features karts which are styled to look like Formula One racing cars. There are high-speed karts for adults, a children's kart circuit for the over 4s, and no danger of selecting the wrong gear, since the karts don't have any. Being low to the ground, they cannot tip over, while at the same time they give a great sensation of speed.

## Fiesta!

(See also p.91). Older children will love the fireworks, devils, dragons (see p.93), and whole exuberant carnival mood of the Catalan celebrations, while

---

### Kids' Stuff in Barcelona

There's plenty for children in Barcelona. The **Barcelona Zoo**, with its famous albino gorilla, and a killer whale and dolphin show, is acclaimed as one of Europe's finest. If the fair seems like more fun, then visit either the **Parc d'Atraccions Montjuïc**, or the **Parc d'Atraccions Tibidabo**. Both have first-class rides and occupy hilltop locations with marvellous views (you'll need a clear day to appreciate Tibidabo). The **cable-car** up to Montjuïc is a wonderful ride in its own right and definitely should not be missed. Tibidabo, which is even higher, is reached by taking the city's last remaining tramcar, the *tramvia blau*, up the hill, where you change to the funicular railway. In terms of funfair attractions, Tibidabo may have the edge.

younger ones will be fascinated by the 4.5m (15ft) 'giants' and cartoon 'big-heads' (see p.93). *Carnaval* itself is a colourful event, though some parents may find its often explicit sensuality unsuitable.

## A Night at the Joust

One of the Costa Maresme's most popular excursions is an evening at the Castell Mediaeval of the Comte de Valltordera. A mediaeval tournament is held while you enjoy a 'mediaeval' dinner.

## Funfairs

Salou has its own permanent funfair, but top of the ratings in every sense are the two in Barcelona (see p.99).

*These carnival creatures look perfectly harmless now, but wait until night-time when they start spitting fire!*

# Shopping

## Shopping Hours

Along the coast, most shops open from about 9am to 2pm and again from 4pm to 8pm or later. Significant exceptions are the big department stores in Barcelona, which no longer observe the siesta.

## Where to Shop

Although you can find almost anything you want in Barcelona, it can be very time consuming to do so, especially when there are so many other marvellous sights to see. You can always combine shopping and sightseeing in the **Poble Espanyol**, where artisans will make a candlestick to order, or blow glass while you wait.

Barcelona has long been an expensive town for shopping, and Sitges is not far behind, while Salou is mostly cheap and cheerful. For individuality and a more reasonable price range, the sidestreets of Tarragona, and the off-the-beaten-track villages and small towns are probably your best bet.

## Best Buys

With the general flattening of prices between Spain and the rest of Europe, genuine good bargains are now few and far between. Aim to come home with something stylish and different, rather than something which is simply cheaper.

**Leatherware**: a cottage industry along the coast produces a multitude of leather goods. Handbags, purses, and clothing are the main items. Price and quality varies widely, so look closely and shop around before buying. The same applies to shoes.

**Jewellery**: either simple, modern designs, or traditional with lots of silver or gold filigree.

**Embroidery, lace, basketwork and woven goods**: there are all kinds of home-spun goods in embroidery, lace and basketwork. You'll generally find them in villages.

**Alcohol and tobacco**: these are still so cheap by European standards that there is no need for duty-free. Take home with you a local drink: a good quality *cava* to remind you of Sant Sadurní d'Anoia; a bottle of the unique Aromes liqueur from Montserrat; or a Moscatel dessert wine – probably as close as you will ever get to capturing Spanish sunshine in a bottle.

**Catalan ceramics**: these may be either primitive or very sophisticated. *Azulejos*, decorative tiles of Moorish origin, are good (if heavy) souvenirs.

**Antiques**: try Barcelona, Sitges or Tarragona. None are cheap, but Tarragona is likely to be the least expensive. Go to the antique market held by the cathedral steps on a Sunday.

# Nightlife

You can find most types of nightlife on the Costa Dorada. It's at its most sophisticated in Barcelona and Sitges, and at its most basic in the mass-market resorts of Salou and Callella. As yet Tarragona has little to offer the tourist.

*A quiet corner of old Tarragona. Buy Roman and mediaeval artefacts from the ceramics shop.*

**Sitges** by night is bohemian and gay in every sense (though by no means exclusively so, see p.34). At weekends it fills up with trendy, young Barceloneses. Discos and disco-bars are always popular, and perhaps the only drawback here is that there are surprisingly few quiet nightspots. The town's most notable disco is Atlántida, principally because it's an open-air venue.

**Salou**, meanwhile, resounds with Euro-pop and karaoke. More up-market is the Galas Nightclub, a dinner and cabaret venue featuring flamenco dancers, Parisian-style showgirls, and the usual cabaret mix. If you are staying on the Costa del Maresme, you are within easy reach of similar entertainment as at the Gran Palace Lloret (at Lloret de Mar on the Costa Brava). You certainly won't be alone at either of these places, as each holds around 1,500 people.

**Barcelona** is one of the world's greatest cities when it comes to nightlife, with entire guidebooks devoted to its plethora of 'designer bars', discos and concert halls. If you don't want to venture out in Barcelona on your own, join an organized coach tour. These depart frequently from Costa Dorada resorts during summer, and after a tour of the floodlit sights of the city, end up at a flamenco show.

## Concerts, Opera, Ballet

If it's the performing arts you want, then a trip to Barcelona is usually necessary. The city's 140-year old Gran Teatre del Liceu is one of Europe's finest theatres, thus tickets are hard to come by. Make enquiries ahead of your intended visit.

Another concert hall worth an admission fee in its own right is the Palau de la Música de Catalana, which is arguably the city's finest example of *Modernisme* architecture.

Aside from these two major venues, there are many more for which tickets are easier to obtain. Ask at a tourist office.

As far from the big city lights as possible is the monastery of Santes Creus (36km/22 miles from Tarragona, see **103** p.81). Performances of classical and church music are occasionally held here in the atmospheric dormitory.

## Cinema

Serious film buffs will know that each October, Sitges hosts an International Festival of Fantasy and Horror Films.

If you want to see a film with its original soundtrack look for the letters 'v.o.' (*version original*).

## Gambling

The only casino on the Costa Dorada is the Gran Casino de Barcelona, which is actually located at San Pere de Ribes, just west of Sitges. Grand it certainly is from the outside, with cypresses, fountains, and gates leading to a 19th-century Catalan-Renaixençe mansion, not unlike an imposing French château in style. The marble foyer is impressive, but the gaming room, slot machines, and decor seem somewhat at odds with the opulence of a previous era.

The casino games you can play here are roulette (European and American), *la boule* (a roulette-style game), *baccara/chemin de fer*, *punto-banco*, and blackjack. Even if you're not gambling, it is fascinating to watch both clients and croupiers at work.

If you intend visiting, you will need either your passport, identity card or driver's licence. A tie isn't necessary, but you should dress smartly. The safest rule for amateurs is to follow the casino's advice – 'stay within your possibilities'. The casino also stages regular international cabaret and occasional outdoor classical music, dance, and opera performances.

If you are staying on the Costa del Maresme, you will be in easy reach of its sister casino, the more modern Casino de Lloret, which offers the same games, albeit in less salubrious surroundings.

Finally, don't confuse the two 'casinos' to be found in Sitges for gaming places. They cashed their chips in long ago and are now cinemas.

# Eating Out

The Catalans take their food seriously, and you will rarely be disappointed by the choice, flavour or hearty portions served up at restaurants along the Costa Dorada. If you don't want a full restaurant meal, there's still plenty of authentic local choice – from *tapas* in a bar, to chicken and *cava* in a fast-food style *pollo a'l ast* (barbecued chicken) outlet.

## Restaurants

Throughout Spain, restaurants are graded by a 'fork' system. One fork is the lowest grade, five forks is the highest. These ratings, however, are awarded according to the facilities and degree of luxury offered, and not the quality of the food. If you're in search of a restaurant that specializes in local food rather than fancy napkins, look out for the sign *tipica* or *típico*. (See p.74 for a list of Recommended Restaurants.)

All restaurants should offer a *menú del dia* (day's special). This is normally three courses, including wine, at a very reasonable set price. The prices on the menu include taxes and a service charge, but it is customary to leave a tip if the service was good.

Two notes of caution: *tapas* prices are not always indicated, and can be surprisingly expensive, so always ask before you order. Also ask how much the bill will be when ordering fish or seafood, priced by the kilo. The price depends on the uncooked weight and can be very expensive.

Meal times are generally later in Spain than in the rest of Europe. Peak hours are generally from 1 to 3.30pm for lunch and 8.30 to 11pm for dinner, although you can get a meal at most places at just about any time of day.

For a comprehensive guide to the vagaries of the menu in Spanish restaurants, there is the Berlitz SPANISH-ENGLISH/ENGLISH-SPANISH POCKET DICTIONARY or the Berlitz EUROPEAN MENU READER.

# Bars and Cafés

From sunrise to the middle of the night, from the first coffee to the last brandy, the Spanish café is a very special institution. In practice there is little difference between what is a bar and what is a café, aside from the bias of the bar towards alcoholic drink.

Bars and cafés are the meeting places for both locals and tourists, either to swap the day's news in pidgin-English, Spanish or German, or shout animatedly at the football on television. The price of a cup of coffee buys you a ring-side seat for as long as you want.

Wines and spirits are served at all hours all over Spain, so don't be surprised if you see someone knocking back a large measure of colourless fire-water first thing in the morning. You may also be surprised to see children frequenting bars with impunity. The Spanish consider this quite natural, even late at night.

Bars and cafés, like restaurants, usually include a service charge, but additional small tips are the custom if you have spent any time in the establishment. Prices are 10-15 percent lower if you stand or sit at the bar rather than occupy a table.

## Tapas

A *tapa* is a small portion of food which encourages you to keep drinking instead of heading off to a restaurant for a more formal meal. The word *tapa* means 'lid', and comes from the old custom of giving a free bite of food with a drink – the food being served on a saucer on top of the glass, like a lid. Nowadays it is rare to see *tapas* given away – perhaps the odd olive or peanut – but bars which specialize in *tapas* are more popular than ever.

Bona-fide *tapas* bars, and indeed many simple bars, have a whole counter display of hot and cold *tapas*, which makes choosing very easy. You can simply point to the one you like the look of. Some of the most common *tapas* you'll find are meatballs, olives, local cheese, Russian salad, *tortilla* (wedges of Spanish omelette),

*A common site in bars – legs of* jamón serrano *and spicy* chorizo *sausages dangling from the ceiling.*

octopus salad, prawns in garlic, mushrooms, *jamón serrano* (mountain-cured ham), and *chorizo* (delicious, spicy, salami-style sausage).

Tapas are always accompanied by a small basket of fresh bread or Catalan-style *pa amb tomaquet* (bread with tomato). The bread is rubbed with garlic, then smeared with tomato, grilled, and then soaked with olive oil.

Portion control: *una tapa* is the smallest amount; *una ración* is half a small plateful, and *una porción* is getting towards a meal in itself. Keep your enthusiasm in check. It is quite easy to spend more on *tapas* than on a good restaurant meal.

**107**

## Breakfast

For Spaniards, breakfast is the least significant meal of the day and will probably just comprise of *tostado* (toast) or *pa amb tomaquet*, and coffee. If you have a sweet tooth, look out for places selling *churros (xurros)*. These are batter fritters, extruded into long strips, deep-fried, and sugared. If you want to be a native, dunk them in your coffee or hot chocolate (more of a thick sauce than drinking chocolate).

Most hotels offer breakfast buffets with an international mélange of cereals, fresh and dried fruits, cheese, cold meats plus bacon and eggs. *Cava* (Spanish champagne) is also sometimes on offer. Several cafés cater for the tourist by

*A* typical Catalan, farmhouse-style restaurant just outside Sitges – rustic decor and guaranteed hearty portions.

offering a full breakfast (*desayuno completo*) of orange juice, bacon, eggs and all the other trimmings.

## Catalan cuisine

There have been several influences on the cuisine of Catalonia and the Costa Dorada. The rich, sauce-based recipes of the South of France filtered down via the Costa Brava, while the abundant rice crops of the Ebro Delta, and Valencia's famous *paellas* wafted up from the south. The sea harvest is a rich source of inspiration, while recipes from the Pyrénées suggest warm, filling peasant food.

There are also national favourites such as *gazpacho* (prononced gath-PATcho), a delicious chilled tomato soup, to which chopped tomatoes, peppers, cucumbers, onions and fried bread croutons are added. Even if the idea of a chilled soup doesn't appeal, try it once, it's a great refresher on a hot summer day.

The classic dish *paella* (pronounced pie-ALE-ya), is named after the black iron pan in which the saffron rice base is cooked in stock. Various combinations of squid, *chorizo*, prawns, shrimps, rabbit, chicken, mussels, onion, peppers, peas and so on are added, according to what type of *paella* is on the menu. It's always cooked to order (usually for a minimum of two people) and is a feast for the eyes as well as the tastebuds. In addition to the above, look out for the following Catalan dishes:

**Bacalao or Bacallà**: salt-cod, surprisingly not a local, but fished from far-off Northern waters. It was salted originally to preserve it, and it's vital that the cod is soaked first to remove the salty taste. Today refrigeration has replaced the salt's preservation role, but salting is still employed in order to impart a distinctive flavour. *Bacallà* is served in numerous ways – one is *Bacallà amb samfaina*, in a sauce resembling ratatouille.

**Escalivada**: an olive-oil dressed cold salad of grilled or **109**

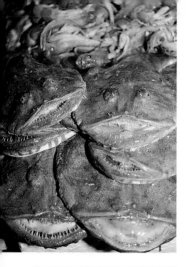

baked vegetables, including peppers and aubergines.

**Escudella**: a hearty meat and vegetable broth with beans, pasta, *chorizo*, chicken or veal. It's not common in tourist haunts, but off the beaten track and out of season you may come across it.

**Esqueixada** (pronounced es-kay-SHA-da): a stimulating salad of salt-cod, red pepper and tomatoes.

**Fideuà**: a plainer cousin of seafood *paella*, substituting noodles for rice and without many of *paella*'s more colourful ingredients.

**Pollo a l'ast**: barbecued chicken hardly qualifies as an authentic Catalan meal, but do look out for these flaming spit-roasted displays, often outside fast-food style establishments. A quarter of a chicken accompanied by a glass of *cava* (more likely to be a plastic cup) is one of the best value meals you can get along the Costa Dorada.

## Fishy Business

The province of Tarragona has long been famous for the quality of its fish, and just as wine has a nominated area quality control, so too does fish.

In this case the denomination is *Peixe Blaue*, literally meaning 'blue fish', although a better translation would be 'blue label'. Look for the crates as they come off the boats, anywhere in the region, and you will see this rating.

**Riz** (or **paella**) **parellada**: a refinement of the normal *paella*. Bones and shells have been sorted, so for the taste without the fuss, it's heaven.

**Romesco**: a sauce that is the pride of Tarragona. It's made of oil, ground almonds, hazelnuts, chilli, tomatoes, garlic, and breadcrumbs, and is perfect for fried fish and shellfish.

**Suquet de Peix**: a rich seafood stew with onions, tomatoes, potatoes, and brandy.

**Xató** (pronounced sha-TO): a salad speciality of Sitges, with anchovies, tuna or cod, and a spicy sauce of oil, vinegar, red pepper, anchovies, garlic and ground almonds, served with olives and endives.

**Zarzuela**: another rich fish and seafood feast in a tomato and wine sauce.

## Dessert

When it comes to dessert, the Catalans seem to lose their inventiveness. *Crema catalana*, made of eggs, sugar, and milk, and flavoured with cinnamon and lemon, is a creamy cousin of the ubiquitous Spanish dessert, *flan*, with a hard, glassy caramelized crust. Aside from these, however, the choice is usually limited to ice-cream (*helado*). If you do get the chance, sample *mel i mató*, a simple (uncooked) mix of honey and fresh cream cheese. It's sold by the market stalls at Montserrat in small tubs, and occasionally finds its way on to restaurant menus.

## Alcoholic Drinks

Both provinces of the Costa Dorada – Barcelona and Tarragona – produce good **wine**. The Penedés region (see p.81) is acclaimed for its excellent still wines, while the region around Sant Sadurni d'Anoía produces more sparkling wine by the *méthode champenoise* than anywhere in the world, including the Champagne region of France itself.

Torres is the most famous label of the Penedés area. This is largely a white wine region **111** but two of the best known Torres labels are on red wines – *Sangre de Toro* ('bull's blood') and the famous, award-winning *Gran Coronas Mas La Plana* (Black Label).

The large *cava* houses are Freixenet and Cordoníu (see p.83), but there are many producers in the region of excellent sparkling wine. *Cava* is not only much cheaper than Champagne, it is also generally less acidic, and therefore appeals to a wider audience. Look for *brut* or *brut natur* on the label if you like it dry.

To the north of Tarragona, the Priorato region is well-known for its full-bodied red wines. Look for *Scala Dei*.

Tarragona and Sitges are known for sweet **dessert wine**. The latter make fortified dessert wines in the same *solera* system used to produce sherry. Try also a Moscatel to accompany your dessert. A good one will have a delicious sultana and honey flavour.

When in Montserratt have a taste of the excellent **liqueur**, *Aromes de Montserrat*, which is made by the monks.

*Sangría* is probably the most popular tourist drink in Spain. It is a mixture of red wine, orange and lemon juice, brandy, and mineral water topped with lots of sliced fruit and ice. Beware, though, this perfect hot weather concoction can pack quite a punch.

**Beer** (*cerveza*) on the Costa Dorada can be any of a number of quality lager brands – *Damm* is recommended. If you want a small beer, ask for *una cerveza pequeña*. *Una cerveza grande* is about the same size as a British pint.

## Tea, Coffee and Soft Drinks

The Spanish usually drink **coffee** (*café*) as opposed to **tea** (*té*). This can be either *solo* (small and black); *con leche* (large with milk, often cappuccino-style); or *cortado* (a small cup with a little milk). Spanish coffee is nearly always strong and tasty. If it is too strong, ask for *Nescafé*, and you'll get a sachet of instant granules and a cup of hot water to make it up to your own strength.

**Mineral water** (*agua mineral*) is either sparkling (*con gas*) or still (*sin gas*). Ice-cream parlours sell *granizado*, slushy, iced fruit juice in several flavours, as well as *zumo de naranjas*, freshly pressed orange juice. The latter is surprisingly expensive given the fact that it is one of Spain's main crops.

You may also come across *horchaterias*, which specialize in the cool, very Spanish refresher, *horchata de chufa*. It's a milky drink made from a fruity, wrinkled little nut with a sweet, almondy taste.

## To Help You Order...

Could we have a table? **¿Nos puede dar una mesa?**
Do you have a set menu? **¿Tiene un menú del día?**
I'd like a/an/some… **Quisiera…**

| | | | |
|---|---|---|---|
| beer | **una cerveza** | potatoes | **patatas** |
| bread | **pan** | salad | **una ensalada** |
| coffee | **un café** | sandwich | **un bocadillo** |
| dessert | **un postre** | soup | **sopa** |
| fish | **pescado** | sugar | **azúcar** |
| ice-cream | **un helado** | tea | **un té** |
| menu | **la carta** | (iced) water | **agua (fresca)** |
| mineral water | **agua mineral** | wine | **vino** |

## ... and read the menu

| | | | |
|---|---|---|---|
| **aceitunas** | olives | **asado** | roast |
| **ajo** | garlic | **atún** | tuna (tunny) |
| **albaricoques** | apricots | **bacalao** | codfish |
| **albóndigas** | meatballs | **besugo** | sea bream |
| **almejas** | baby clams | **bistec** | beef steak |
| **anchoas** | anchovies | **boquerones** | fresh |
| **anguila** | eel | | anchovies |
| **arroz** | rice | **caballa** | mackerel |

**113**

| | | | |
|---|---|---|---|
| **calamares** | squid | **langostino** | prawn |
| **(a la romana)** | (deep fried) | **lenguado** | sole |
| **callos** | tripe | **limón** | lemon |
| **cangrejo** | crab | **lomo** | loin |
| **caracoles** | snails | **manzana** | apple |
| **cebollas** | onions | **mariscos** | shellfish |
| **cerdo** | pork | **mejillones** | mussels |
| **champiñones** | mushrooms | **melocotón** | peach |
| **chorizo** | a spicy pork sausage | **merluza** | hake |
| | | **naranja** | orange |
| **chuleta** | chops | **ostras** | oysters |
| **cordero** | lamb | **pastel** | cake |
| **dorada** | seabass | **pescado** | fish |
| **ensalada** | salad | **pescadilla** | whiting |
| **entremeses** | hors-d'oeuvre | **pez espada** | swordfish |
| **estofado** | stew | **pimiento** | green pepper |
| **filete** | fillet | **piña** | pineapple |
| **flan** | crème caramel | **plátano** | banana |
| | | **pollo** | chicken |
| **frambuesas** | raspberries | **postre** | dessert |
| **fresas** | strawberries | **pulpitos** | baby octopus |
| **frito** | fried | **queso** | cheese |
| **galletas** | biscuits (cookies) | **salchichón** | salami-type sausage |
| **gambas** | shrimp | **salmonete** | red mullet |
| **granadas** | pomegranates | **salsa** | sauce |
| **guisantes** | peas | **sandía** | watermelon |
| **helado** | ice-cream | **sopa** | soup |
| **hígado** | liver | **ternera** | veal |
| **higos** | figs | **tortilla** | omelet |
| **huevo** | eggs | **tostada** | toast |
| **jamón** | ham | **trucha** | trout |
| **judías** | beans | **uvas** | grapes |
| **114 langosta** | spiny lobster | **verduras** | vegetables |

# BLUEPRINT
## for a
## Perfect Trip

# An A–Z Summary of Practical Information

## A

**ACCOMMODATION** (see also CAMPING on p.117, YOUTH HOSTELS on p.141and the list of RECOMMENDED HOTELS starting on p.66).

Most accommodation in the Costa Dorada is of a medium international standard, with a predominance of two- and three-star hotels. Hotels are the norm, but apartments and aparthotels may be found in the more popular coastal resorts. Hotels are government-inspected and graded 1–5 stars depending upon facilities. Hostels (*hostales*) are modest hotels with few facilities and are denoted by the sign **Hs**. Pensions (*pensiones*, boarding houses denoted by the letter **P**) are the most basic form of accommodation. Both *pensiones* and *hostales* are graded 1–3 stars. The letter **R**, suffixed to a hotel or hostel sign, indicates *residencia*. In theory this means that there is no restaurant and the establishment does bed-and-breakfast only, but this is not always the case.

Spain's most notable accommodation is usually found in *paradores*. These are state-run establishments, sometimes set in historic buildings, or sometimes in functional modern blocks in outstanding surroundings. Their aim is to provide the chance to experience 'the real Spain' and to reflect the indigenous style. The only *parador* on the Costa Dorada is at Tortosa.

Most accommodation in resorts such as Salou is in reasonably priced 2–3-star hotels and apartments. Sitges, on the other hand, caters for a more chic crowd, including weekend Barceloneses, and is therefore quite expensive. The Costa del Maresme resorts are also popular with Barceloneses. Barcelona itself is very expensive and Tarragona suffers from a dearth of accommodation. As a general rule, book ahead whenever possible.

When booking for any accommodation, you will be asked to surrender your passport for a short period. In general, prices are quoted per room (as opposed to per person). Value added tax (IVA) of 6% is added to the bill (13% at 5-star hotels).

| | |
|---|---|
| a single/double room | **una habitación individual/ doble** |
| with bath/shower | **con baño/ducha** |
| What's the rate per night? | **¿Cuál es el precio por noche?** |

## AIRPORTS (aeropuerto)

Charter flights for resorts near Tarragona use the modest airport at Reus, 19km (12 miles) north of Tarragona. Barcelona's modern and stylish airport is at El Prat de Llobregat, 15km (9 miles) from the city centre. It has all the facilities you would expect of an important international airport and is linked to the city by a regular train service.

For the best selection and prices, buy any tobacco and alcohol that you intend taking home at the supermarket, rather than at the airport duty-free shops.

C

## CAMPING (camping)

The Costa Dorada has more officially approved campsites than any other resort area in Spain. Ask the Spanish Tourist Board to send you their *Guia Càmpings Catalunya*, or apply to the Federació Catalana de Campings, Via Laietana, 59, Barcelona; tel. 317 4416.

Camping grounds are divided into four categories (luxury, 1st-, 2nd- and 3rd-class) and rates and facilities vary accordingly. All sites have drinking water, toilets and showers, electricity, medical facilities, and safes for valuables, and are attended night and day.

| | |
|---|---|
| We have a tent/caravan (trailer). | **Tenemos una tienda de camping/una caravana**. |

**117**

**CAR HIRE** (*coches de alquiler*) (see also Dʀɪᴠɪɴɢ on p.123)

Car hire firms on the Costa Dorada offer a wide range of cars at varying prices. Always shop around for the best deal. If you want to book in advance, try Holiday Autos (tel. 071-491 1111), Europe's largest car rental brokers. They guarantee the lowest hire prices and always use reputable local companies. If you are flying into Barcelona, a good local hire company is Thrifty, Avenida Sarria, 32, 08029 Barcelona; tel. 430 90 71.

Third-party insurance is always included in the basic charge and so usually is CDW (Collision Damage Waiver). Personal accident insurance is normally covered by your own standard travel insurance policy.

You must be over 21 if you are paying by credit card and over 23 if you are paying by cash. In the latter case an additional deposit may be required. Although officially you should have an International Driving Permit, in practice, driving licences from all major countries are accepted without question.

| | |
|---|---|
| I'd like to hire a car (tomorrow). | **Quisiera alquilar un coche (para mañana).** |
| for one day/week | **por un día/una semana** |
| Please include full insurance. | **Haga el favor de incluir el seguro a todo riesgo.** |

## CLIMATE

Sunbathers can enjoy the beaches of the Costa Dorada for about five months of the year. The mild climate throughout the rest of the year

|         |     | J  | F  | M  | A  | M  | J  | J  | A  | S  | O  | N  | D  |
|---------|-----|----|----|----|----|----|----|----|----|----|----|----|----|
| maximum | °F  | 55 | 57 | 60 | 65 | 71 | 78 | 82 | 82 | 77 | 69 | 62 | 56 |
|         | °C  | 13 | 14 | 16 | 18 | 21 | 25 | 28 | 28 | 25 | 21 | 16 | 13 |
| minimum | °F  | 43 | 45 | 48 | 52 | 57 | 65 | 69 | 69 | 66 | 58 | 51 | 46 |
|         | °C  | 6  | 7  | 9  | 11 | 14 | 18 | 21 | 21 | 19 | 15 | 11 | 8  |

still provides a pleasant break from chilly Northern Europe and is ideal for sports.

Minimum temperatures are measured just before sunrise, maximum temperatures in the afternoon.

## CLOTHING

In addition to summer- and beach-wear, don't forget sweaters or wraps for evenings. For the excursion to Montserrat (see p.60) you may need warmer clothing (though walking will soon warm you up) and sturdy shoes.

Casual wear is the norm, though if you intend to frequent expensive hotels or restaurants, the opera house, theatre or the casino, then a jacket and tie (though not obligatory) may be required.

Topless bathing has become quite common, but you must cover up off the beach. Bermuda shorts and mini-skirts should not be worn when visiting religious sites.

## COMPLAINTS

By law, all hotels and restaurants must have official complaint forms (*Hojas de Reclamación*) and are obliged to produce them on demand. The original of this document should be sent to the Ministry of Tourism, one copy remains with the establishment involved, and one copy is given to the person who is making the complaint.

Try to resolve the problem before going through this procedure, as in practice it is difficult to pursue any claims once you have left the area. The very action of asking for the *hoja*, however, may resolve the problem in itself, as tourism authorities often view malpractice seriously, and can revoke or suspend licences.

The Catalan Regional Tourist Board has also set up a telephone line which acts as an advisory service on any complaints you may have; tel. 900-30 03 03 (calls are free).

You should also inform the local tourist office, or in serious cases the local police, of any complaints, and seek their assistance. **119**

## CONSULATES (consulado)

The consulates listed below are all in Barcelona, which is also the location of consulates representing almost all other Western European countries. Citizens of Commonwealth countries may also call on the UK consulate. All embassies are located in Madrid.

If you run into trouble with the authorities or the police, contact your consulate for advice.

**Canada**: Via Augusta, 125; tel. 209 06 34

**Eire**: 10th Floor, Gran Via Carles III, 94; tel. 330 96 52

**South Africa**: Avenida da Roma, 94-96; tel. 453 19 68

**UK**: Avinguda Diagonal, 477; tel. 322 21 51

**USA**: Paseo Rheina Elisenda, 23; tel. 280 22 27

There is also an honorary UK consulate in Tarragona at: Carrer Reial, 33, 1r.1a; tel. 22 08 12.

| | |
|---|---|
| Where is the British/ American consulate? | **¿Dónde ésta el consulado británico/americano?** |
| It's very urgent. | **Es muy urgente**. |

## CRIME (see also Lost Property on p.130)

The most common crime against the tourist in Spain is theft from hire cars. If you park overnight in the street in one of the big towns or resorts, there is every chance that your car will be broken into.

Thieves also operate at tourist locations where cars are left unattended. Never leave anything of value in your car at any time. Hotels recommend that you use the safe deposit box in your room – for which there is usually a charge – for all valuables, including your passport. Burglaries at holiday apartments do occur, so keep doors and windows locked when you are absent and while you are asleep.

Beware of pickpockets, particularly in crowded places, such as markets or bus stations, or on the Barcelona Metro. If you are visiting Barcelona, be particularly vigilant on the lower section of Las

Ramblas (beware of street sellers). You must report all thefts to the local police for your own insurance purposes.

On a more cheerful note, crimes involving violence against tourists are rare.

I want to report a theft. **Quiero denunciar un robo**.

## CUSTOMS AND ENTRY FORMALITIES

Most visitors, including citizens of all EC countries, the USA, Canada, Eire, Australia, and New Zealand, require only a valid passport – no visa, no health certificate – to enter Spain. Visitors from South Africa must have a visa.

If you expect to remain for longer than 90 days (US citizens 180 days), a Spanish consulate or tourist office can advise you.

Although there is no restriction on what you may bring in with you as a tourist, you will find the same items much cheaper in Spain.

The following chart shows the main duty-free items that you are allowed to take back into your own country:

| Into: | Cigarettes | | Cigars | | Tobacco | Spirits | | Wine |
|---|---|---|---|---|---|---|---|---|
| Spain 1) | 200 | or | 50 | or | 250 g | 1 l | or | 2 l |
| Australia | 200 | or | 250 | or | 250 g | 1 l | or | 1 l |
| Canada | 200 | and | 50 | and | 900 g | 1.1 l | or | 1.1 l |
| N.Zealand | 200 | or | 50 | or | 250 g | 1.1 l | and | 4.5 l |
| S.Africa | 400 | and | 50 | and | 250 g | 1 l | and | 2 l |
| U.S.A. | 200 | and | 100 | and | 2) | 1 l | or | 1 l |
| Within the EC 3) | 800 | and | 200 | and | 1kg | 10 l | and | 90 l |

1) Arriving from non-EC countries, or EC countries with duty-free.
2) A reasonable quantity.
3) Guidelines for non duty-free within the EC. For the import of larger amounts you must be able to prove that the goods are for your own personal use. For EC duty-free allowances see 1) above.

**Currency restrictions**. Tourists may bring an unlimited amount of Spanish or foreign currency into the country and take out (undeclared) up to the equivalent of 1 million pesetas.

| | |
|---|---|
| I've nothing to declare. | **No tengo nada que declarar**. |
| It's for my personal use. | **Es para mi uso personal**. |

## D

## DISABLED TRAVELLERS

In general, provisions for wheelchair travellers on the Costa Dorada are not particularly good. Following the Barcelona Paralympics of 1992, however, awareness of the needs of the disabled traveller has at least been raised.

There are wheelchair ramps at the airports, and many larger apartments and hotels make provision for disabled guests. Salou has by far the greatest number of hotels – 14 in all – with wheelchair facilities. Another three in Cambrils also claim facilities. Aside from these, there are a few other wheelchair-friendly establishments, most of which are provided by Best Western Hotels; tel. 081 541 0033 for more details. Youth hostels at Deltebre, El Masnou (Costa del Maresme), and Barcelona are also suitable for wheelchair users.

Further details of accessible accommodation are given in *Holidays and Travel Abroad*, published by RADAR, 25 Mortimer Street, London W1N 8AB; tel. 071 637 5400. (see also the list of RECOMMENDED HOTELS starting on p.66).

Other sources of information are the Spanish National Tourist Office and the Federation ECOM, which is a group of private organizations for the disabled; Gran Via de las Corts Catalanes 562-2a, 08011, Barcelona. They also publish an Access guide to Barcelona.

Finally, before you go, contact the Holiday Care Service, who are experts in the field of holidays for disabled people and will try to answer specific queries; tel. (0293) 774 535.

## DRIVING

**Arrival**. If you want to bring your own car to Spain, you will need the car registration papers, a nationality plate or sticker, a red warning triangle, a Green Card extension to your regular insurance policy, and a bail bond which can also be arranged through your insurance company. You will also require an International Driving Permit.

**Driving conditions**. Drive on the right, overtake on the left, and yield right of way to all vehicles coming from your right.

Main roads are very good and even country roads are well surfaced. The A7 *autopista* (motorway) winds inland from Barcelona before heading south west, parallel to the coast, all the way to the Costa del Azahar. This is an excellent, fast road, but beware of hefty tolls and the fact that many junctions do not allow both entrance and exit. If you do intend using the *autopista*, it's worth looking for a map which gives details on junction restrictions or you can be stuck on the motorway for several miles before you can exit. Beware, too, of driving anywhere on a Sunday evening. Massive traffic jams build up, both on and off the motorway, as Barcelonan weekenders head back from the beach.

Driving and parking is tolerable in Tarragona, but is certainly not recommended in the centre of Barcelona, although a new through-road system has greatly improved the journey across the city. It is advisable to study maps carefully before setting off.

**Parking**. Metered parking is quite common in both large and small towns. Your car will be towed away if you park illegally in Barcelona. It is an offence to park the car facing against the traffic.

**Traffic police**. Armed civil guards (*Guardia Civil*) patrol the roads on powerful black motorcycles. In towns the municipal police handle traffic control. If you are fined for a traffic offence, you will have to pay on the spot.

**Rules and regulations**. Always carry your driving licence and/or International Driving Permit with you. As the police can demand to see **123**

your passport at any time, it is also a good idea to carry a photocopy of its important pages (if not the actual passport itself) with you.

Spanish law requires that your car should carry a set of spare head-lamp and rear-lamp bulbs. Motorcyclists and pillion riders must wear crash helmets and motor- cycle lights must always be switched on. Seat belts are compulsory when driving outside built-up city areas. Children under the age of ten must travel in the rear.

**Breakdowns**. Spanish garages are efficient and spare parts are readily available for most makes of car. If you are an affiliated member of the RAC, you may call on the services of the *Reial Automòbil Club de Catalunya*, who are at: Santaló 8, 08008 Barcelona; tel. 200 33 11; and Rambla Nova 114, Tarragona; tel. 21 19 62. *ADAC*, a motoring organization affiliated to the AA, can be found at Carre Muntaner, 239-253, Barcelona; tel. 200 88 00.

**Road signs**. Aside from the standard pictographs you may encounter the following:

| | |
|---|---|
| **Aparcamiento** | Parking |
| **Autopista (de peaje/peatge)** | (Toll) motorway (expressway) |
| **Ceda el paso** | Give way (Yield) |
| **Despacio** | Slow |
| **Desviación** | Diversion (Detour) |
| **Estacionamiento prohibido** | No parking |

| | |
|---|---|
| **Obras** | Roadworks |
| **¡Pare!** | Stop |
| **Peatones** | Pedestrians |
| **Peligro** | Danger |
| **Sortida** | Exit (from motorway/expressway) |
| Driving licence | **Carné de conducir** |
| Car registration papers | **Permiso de circulación** |
| Green card | **Carta verde** |
| Can I park here? | **¿Se puede aparcar aqui?** |
| Are we on the right road for…? | **¿Es ésta la carretera hacia…?** |
| Fill the tank please, top grade. | **Llénelo, por favor, con super.** |
| Check the oil/tires/battery. | **Por favor, controle el aceite/los neumáticos/la batería.** |
| I've broken down. | **Mi coche se ha estropeado.** |
| There's been an accident. | **Ha habido un accidente.** |

# E

## ELECTRIC CURRENT (*corriente eléctrica*)

220-volt current is the norm, though if you are in an old building in the countryside, you may find 125-volt current. If in doubt, ask.

If you have trouble with an appliance ask your desk clerk or courier to recommend an *electricista*.

| | |
|---|---|
| What's the voltage – 125 or 220? | **¿Cuál es el voltaje – ciento veinticinco (125) o doscientos veinte (220)?** |
| a battery | **una pila** |

**EMERGENCIES** (*urgencia*) (see also CONSULATES on p.120,
MEDICAL CARE on p.131, and POLICE on p.135)

If your hotel desk clerk isn't available to help, here are a few emergency numbers:

| | |
|---|---|
| Municipal police | **091 (092** in Barcelona) |
| Civil Guard | **062** |
| Red Cross Tarragona | **23 83 32** |

And a few phrases we hope you won't have to use...

| | |
|---|---|
| Fire | **Fuego** |
| Help | **Socorro** |
| Police | **Policía** |
| Stop | **Deténgase** |
| Stop thief! | **¡Al ladrón!** |

## ETIQUETTE

The Catalans are an easy-going, friendly people. In the countryside and smaller towns many still share a belief in the virtues of *mañana*; don't try to rush them. Far from making things better, it might well lengthen the delay. Barceloneses are different. They are altogether more dynamic, more European, but no less friendly. The Tarragonese, meanwhile, are somewhere in between the two.

In a restaurant, you must always ask for the bill (*la cuenta, por favor*). It is very rarely offered, because no waiter wants to be seen to be actually encouraging you to leave.

Politeness and simple courtesies still matter. Always begin a conversation with *buenos dias* ('good morning') or *buenas tardes* ('good afternoon'), and sign off with *adiós* ('goodbye') or *buenas noches* ('goodnight') when leaving. A pleasant way of greeting someone is to ask, *¿Cómo ésta usted?* ('How are you?'), or if asked the same question yourself, to reply, *Muy bien, gracias* ('Very well, thank you').

## GETTING TO THE COSTA DORADA

**BY AIR** (see also AIRPORTS on p.116)
If you are visiting the Costa Dorada on a charter flight, you will fly into Reus. Scheduled flights go to Barcelona. However don't assume that charter flights are always the cheapest. Iberia, the national airline, does offer very competitive prices at most times of the year, and a more comfortable, flexible service. Check with them on 071-830 0011. Iberia only fly to Barcelona. The flight from London to Barcelona or Reus takes 2 hours.

Transatlantic travellers usually enter Spain via Madrid Airport.

**BY ROAD**
The main access road from France to the Costa Dorada is at the eastern side of the Pyrenées. You can join the A7 *autopista* at the frontier post of La Jonquera, 150km (93 miles) north of Barcelona. An alternative route from Toulouse, over the Pyrenées, enters Spain at Puigcerdà and follows the N152 route for 169km (105 miles) to Barcelona. The scenic route is the coast road from the Port Bou border post along the Costa Brava.

Alternatively, there is a choice of two ferry crossings to northern Spain. Brittany Ferries operate between Plymouth and Santander (24 hours), while P&O run from Portsmouth to Bilbao (28-29 hours). From Santander or Bilbao it's an 8- to 9-hour drive to Barcelona on the N240. Coaches take 26 hours from London to Barcelona, then continue south to Valencia. Enquire about stopping at Tarragona.

**BY RAIL**
The Barcelona–Talgo links Paris with Barcelona in about 12 hours. From there, change at Sants Station for the coastal line to Tarragona and beyond. For most other connections, you'll have to change trains at Port Bou.

Both Inter-Rail and Rail Europ Senior cards are valid in Spain. Non-European residents should enquire about the Eurailpass before **127** they leave home. The Freedom Pass from Euro-Domino offers travel on any 3, 5 or 10 days within one month in several European countires. For further enquiries write or call at the International Rail Centre, Victoria Station, London SW1Y 1JY, or telephone 071-834 2345. The Spanish National Railways, RENFE (*Red Nacional de los Ferrocariles Española*) also offer unlimited rail travel passes.

## GUIDES and TOURS

Tour operators run coaches on various day trips along the Costa Dorada. Depending on where you are staying, you will be able to choose from the following: Poblet and Santes Creus, Tarragona, Barcelona (by day and by night), Montserrat (combined with a visit to a *cava* producer), Andorra, and Peñiscola (Costa del Azahar). Costa Maresme operators also run several trips to the Costa Brava. Commentaries are given in all major languages, though it never harms to specify the language you require at the time of booking.

Tours can be booked through your hotel reception and most travel agents. If you would like a personal guide to a particular place, the tourist office should be able to direct you to local guides and tell you their rates.

| | |
|---|---|
| We'd like an English-speaking guide. | **Queremos un guía que hable inglés.** |

## L

**LANGUAGE** (see also Maps and Street Names on p.130)

Both Catalan and Castilian Spanish are official languages in Catalonia. Catalan is a Romance language, with its roots in the French Langue d'Oc, which originated in the Provence area of France. The most intimidating part is trying to pronounce all those words with 'x' in them (as 'Óch' or 'Ósh', as in *anxoves* – 'anchovies').

Regional policy and the personal preference of most Catalans is towards Catalan, but don't worry – the people you meet will speak to you in Spanish (or your own language). Street signs are in Catalan, museum captions and menus are usually in both languages.

It may be possible to get through your holiday without any Spanish, since in tourist areas, French, English, Italian and German are often spoken, or at least understood. Nevertheless, learning and using some courtesy phrases in Catalan will always go down well.

| English | Catalan | Castilian |
|---|---|---|
| Good morning/Good day | **Bon dia** | **Buenos días** |
| Good afternoon/Good evening | **Bona tarda** | **Buenas tardes** |
| Goodnight | **Bona nit** | **Buenas noches** |
| Please | **Si us plau** | **Por favor** |
| Thank you | **Gràcies** | **Gracias** |
| You're welcome | **De res** | **De nada** |
| Goodbye | **Adéu** | **Adiós** |

The Berlitz phrasebook SPANISH FOR TRAVELLERS covers most situations you are likely to encounter during your travels in Spain. In addition the Berlitz Spanish-English/English-Spanish pocket dictionary also contains a menu-reader supplement.

There is a list of useful expressions on the cover of this guide, but here are a few more that may come in handy:

| | |
|---|---|
| where/when/how | **dónde/cuándo/cómo** |
| how long/how far | **cuánto tiempo/a qué distancia** |
| yesterday/today/tomorrow | **ayer/hoy/mañana** |
| day/week/month/year | **día/semana/mes/año** |
| left/right | **izquierda/derecha** |
| up/down | **arriba/abajo** |
| good/bad | **bueno/malo** |
| big/small | **grande/pequeño** |

| | | |
|---|---|---|
| cheap/expensive | **barato/caro** | |
| hot/cold | **caliente/frío** | |
| old/new | **viejo/nuevo** | |

## LOST PROPERTY

Retrace your steps. If you still cannot find the missing item, report the loss to the Municipal Police or the Guardia Civil (see POLICE on p.135). They will issue you with a form which you will need a copy of if you wish to make an insurance claim once you are home.

To report a lost credit card, phone American Express (217-0070), Eurocard (302-1428), Mastercard or Visa (315-2512)

| | |
|---|---|
| I've lost my wallet/ handbag/passport. | **He perdido mi cartera/ bolso/pasaporte.** |

## MAPS and STREET NAMES

One manifestation of the upheavals that post-Franco Catalonia has been undergoing is in the name of streets, many of which are being re-baptized, causing some confusion. Place, street and even people's names in Catalonia are mostly met with today in their Catalan version, eg. San Carlos is now Sant Carles, Jaime is Jaume, Pablo is Pau, Lérida is Lleida, and so on. Here are a few Catalan street signs:

| *English* | *Catalan* | *Castilian* |
|---|---|---|
| Avenue | **Avinguda** | **Avenida** |
| Street | **Carrer** | **Calle** |
| Church | **Església** | **Iglesia** |
| Palace | **Palau** | **Palacio** |
| Boulevard | **Passeig** | **Paseo** |
| Square | **Plaça** | **Plaza** |

| | |
|---|---|
| a street plan of… | **un plano de la ciudad de…** |
| a road map of… | **mapa de carreteras de…** |

## MEDICAL CARE

EC residents should obtain form E111, which entitles them to free medical treatment within the EC. It is unwise to travel without health insurance as treatment can be expensive.

Many tourists from northern climes often suffer painful sunburn through overdoing it on the first day or two. Falling asleep on the beach is a common cause. Take the sun in short doses for at least the first few days, and go steady on the alcohol as well. Spirits are poured in liver-crippling measures and the beer also packs a punch. Drink plenty of bottled water (*agua mineral*) to avoid dehydration.

A list of doctors who speak your language is available at local tourist offices. There are hospitals in all the principal towns and a first-aid station (*casa de socorro*) in smaller places.

**Chemist's** (*farmacia*) are recognisable by a green cross sign and are open during normal shopping hours. After hours, at least one per town – the *farmacia de guardia* – remains open all night. Its address is posted in the window of the other *farmacias*.

| | |
|---|---|
| Where's the nearest (all-night) pharmacy? | **¿Dónde ésta la farmacia (de guardia) más cercana?** |
| I need a doctor/dentist. | **Necesito un médico/dentista.** |
| I've a pain here. | **Me duele aquí.** |
| sunburn | **quemadura del sol** |
| sunstroke | **insolación** |
| a fever | **fiebre** |
| an upset stomach | **molestias de estómago** |
| insect bite | **una picadura de insecto** |

**131**

## MONEY MATTERS

**Currency**. The monetary unit of Spain is the *peseta* (abbreviated pta). Coins come in 1, 5, 10, 25, 50, 100, 200 and 500 pesetas. Banknotes come in 100, 500, 1,000, 2,000 and 5,000 pesetas. For currency restrictions see CUSTOMS AND ENTRY FORMALITIES on p.121.

**Banking hours** are usually from 9am to 2pm Monday to Friday. Banks in the popular resorts also open longer hours and on Saturday at the height of the season. Beware of hefty transaction charges.

Outside banking hours, many travel agencies display a *cambio* sign and will change foreign currency. Most hotels will also change money, albeit at a slightly less favourable rate than at the bank.

**Traveller's cheques** always get a better rate than cash. Take your passport with you when changing money or traveller's cheques.

**Credit cards**, **traveller's cheques** and **Eurocheques** are accepted in most hotels, restaurants and big shops.

| | |
|---|---|
| Where's the nearest bank? | **¿Dónde está el banco más cercano?** |
| I want to change some pounds. | **Quiero cambiar libras.** |
| Do you accept traveller's cheques? | **¿Acepta usted cheques de viaje?** |
| Can I pay with this credit card? | **¿Puedo pagar con esta tarjeta de crédito?** |

# N

## NEWSPAPERS AND MAGAZINES (*periódico; revista*)

Major British and Continental newspapers are on sale the same day as publication.

| | |
|---|---|
| Have you any English-language newspapers? | **¿Tiene periódicos en inglés?** |

## OPENING HOURS

These vary, but generally work around the siesta, with whole towns and villages literally going to sleep during the mid-afternoon.

**Banks**. 9am to 2pm Monday to Friday.

**Bars and restaurants**. It is difficult to generalize, but in the resorts many bars open from noon or earlier until the small hours. Similarly, less formal restaurants open all day.

**Museums**. Times are variable, but most open between 10am and 1 to 2pm, and re-open from 3 or 4pm to 6 or 7pm. However, some go straight through from 10am to 5.30pm. Most close all day Monday.

**Post Offices**. Provincial offices open from 8 or 9am to noon or 1pm, and 4 or 5pm to 6 or 7pm Monday to Friday. Most open mornings only on Saturday. Tarragona's main office opens 8am to 9pm.

**Shops**. 9am to 1pm, and 4 or 5pm to 7 or 8pm, Monday to Saturday.

## PHOTOGRAPHY

All popular brands and types of film, camera batteries, flash batteries, and general accessories are sold on the Costa Dorada at competitive prices. One-day processing is widely available for print films.

Field workers, fishermen, and peasants can make very photogenic subjects, but wherever possible, ask for their permission before you take their picture. Most do not mind and are often quite amused, but some older folk will turn away. Do not harass them.

It is forbidden to take photographs of any military bases, military or naval port areas, police, government, or military personnel.

| | |
|---|---|
| I'd like a film for this camera. | **Quisiera un carrete para está máquina**. |

## PLANNING YOUR BUDGET

The following list will give you some idea of prices on the Costa Dorada. Prices continually change however, and while these were correct at the time of going to press, they must be regarded as approximate and vulnerable to inflation.

**Attractions**. Waterparks around 4,000 ptas per adult, 2,400 ptas per child.

**Babysitters**. From 500 ptas per hour.

**Beach equipment hire**. Two beds and sunshade 1,000-1,400 ptas per day.

**Bicycle hire**. From 1,700 ptas per day.

**Camping**. Average 450 ptas per person plus 450 ptas per tent.

**Car hire**. Rates vary widely. The following is an average of local companies. Group A (*Seat Marbella*) 1-3 days, 3,300 ptas per day, 7 days 20,000 ptas. Group B (*Opel Corsa/Renault 5*) 1-3 days, 3,400 ptas per day, 7 days 22,000 ptas. Group C (*Opel Kadett/Ford Fiesta/Ford Escort*) 1-3 days 4,500 ptas per day, 7 days 28,000 ptas.

**Excursions**. Barcelona highlights 3,000 ptas; Montserrat 2,800 ptas; Andorra 3,900 ptas; Galas Night Club, Salou 3,300 ptas (all prices include lunch or dinner).

Independent travel: Barcelona Bus Turistic 1,000 ptas. Cable-car and funiculars at Montserrat 650-700 ptas per ride.

**Hotels** (double room with bath/shower, low to high season). There are great variations according to resorts. The following reflect prices around Tarragona: 4-star 8,500-25,000 ptas; 3-star 6,000-20,000 ptas; 2-star 4,500-8,000 ptas.

**Meals and drinks**. Continental breakfast from 500 ptas; *menu del día* from 1,000 ptas; three-course lunch/dinner (excluding wine) in a fairly good establishment, around 2,700 ptas. Coffee from 125 ptas; beer (local) from 150 ptas; soft drink from 125 ptas.

**Motorway tolls**. 230-460 ptas.

**Museums**. 100-400 ptas, sometimes free.

**Nightlife**. Casino admission 550 ptas, discothèque from 600 ptas (includes first drink).

**Petrol**. 96 ptas per litre.

**Shopping**. Bread (250g) 70 ptas, butter (250g) from 250 ptas, pork/veal (per kilo) 700-1,200 ptas, instant Nescafé coffee (200g) 680 ptas, bottle of wine from 220 ptas, fruit juice (1 litre) from 200 ptas, milk (1 litre) from 100 ptas.

**Sports**. *Golf*. Green fee 4,500-7,000 ptas per day, club hire from 2,000 ptas. *Horse-riding* from 1,600 ptas per hour. *Tennis* from 500 ptas per hour. *Water-skiing* (one turn) 1,800 ptas. W*indsurfing* 1,500 ptas per hour. *Parascending* 3,500 ptas. *'Water sausage'* 600 ptas.

**Taxis**. Flat charge of 225 ptas plus 80 ptas per kilometre.

## POLICE (*policía*)

There are three police forces in Spain. The best known is the *Guardia Civil* (Civil Guard). Each town also has its own *Policía Municipal* (municipal police) who wear a different uniform depending on the town and season, but are mostly found in blue and grey. The third force, the *Cuerpo Nacional de Policía*, a national anti-crime unit, can be recognized by their light brown uniforms. All policemen are armed. If you need police assistance you can call on any of these forces.

Where is the nearest police station? **¿Dónde está la comisaria más cercana?**

## POST OFFICES

These are for mail and telegrams, not telephone calls. Stamps (*sellos* or *timbres*) are sold at any tobacconists (*tabacos*) and by most shops which sell postcards.

**Post boxes** are painted yellow. The slot marked *estrangers* is for overseas mail.

**Poste restante** (general delivery): If you don't know in advance where you will be staying, you can still have mail forwarded to you addressed poste restante (*lista de correos*), at whichever town is most convenient, ie: Mr John Smith, Lista de Correos, Tarragona, Spain.

When collecting you must take your passport to the post office as identification.

| | |
|---|---|
| Where is the (nearest) post office? | **¿Dónde está la oficina de correos (más cercana)?** |
| Have you received any mail for…? | **¿Ha recibido correo para...?** |
| A stamp for this letter/postcard please. | **Por favor, un sello para esta carta/tarjeta.** |
| express (special delivery) | **urgente** |
| airmail | **via aérea** |
| registered | **certificado** |
| I want to send a telegram to… | **Quisiera mandar un telegramma a…** |

## PUBLIC HOLIDAYS (*fiesta*)

| | | |
|---|---|---|
| January 1 | *Año Nuevo* | New Year's Day |
| January 6 | *Epifanía* | Epiphany |
| May 1 | *Día del Trabajo* | Labour Day |
| June 24 | *Día de Santa Joan* | St John's Day |
| July 25 | *Santiago Apóstol* | St James' Day |
| August 15 | *Asunción* | Assumption |
| October 12 | *Día de la Hispanidad* | Discovery of America Day (Columbus Day) |
| November 1 | *Todos los Santos* | All Saints' Day |

| December 6 | *Día de la Constitución Española* | Constitution Day |
| December 25 | *Navidad* | Christmas Day |
| December 26 | *San Esteban* | St Stephen's Day |

**Movable dates**

| Jueves Santo | *Maundy Thursday* | |
| Viernes Santo | *Good Friday* | |
| Lunes de Pascua | *Easter Monday* | |
| Corpus Christi | *Corpus Christi* | |
| Inmaculada Concepción | *Immaculate Conception* | (normally December 8) |

In addition to these Spanish national holidays, many other purely local holidays are celebrated in various towns (see FESTIVALS AND FOLKLORE on p.91).

Are you open tomorrow?   **¿Está abierto mañana?**

## PUBLIC TRANSPORT

**Bus services**. Buses are cheap, reasonably comfortable and reliable, but beware of drastically reduced timetables on Sunday. They generally only run into and out of the provincial centres, so links to smaller resorts, even if they are quite close to each other, may not be possible. There are regular buses from Tarragona to Salou and Cambrils (15-20 mins), Poblet (75 mins), Montblanc (60 mins) and Barcelona (90 mins).

**Train services**. A good service, linking all the main resorts and towns, runs right down the Costa del Maresme, through Barcelona, and along the Costa Dorada to Valencia. There are several different types of train. The slowest and local services are called *Semi-directo*, *Tranvía*, *Omnibus* or *Automotor*. These are no faster than the bus. *Expreso* and *Rápido* are long-distance expresses, while *Talgo*, *Intercity*, *Electrotren*, *Ter*, and *Tren Estrella* are luxury long-distance **137**

expresses. The expresses offer first and second-class compartments. The Barcelona station serving the coastal line is Sants.

| | |
|---|---|
| When is the next bus/train for…? | **¿A qué hora sale el próximo autobús/tren para…?** |
| I want a ticket to… | **Quiero un billete para…** |
| What's the fare to…? | **¿Cuánto es la tarifa a …?** |
| first/second class | **primera/segunda clase** |
| single (one-way) | **ida** |
| return (round-trip) | **ida y vuelta** |

## R

## RADIO and TV (*radio; televisión*)

Most hotels have television lounges where Spanish and satellite channels are broadcast. There are seven Spanish channels, most dedicated largely to sport, foreign films and game-shows. Travellers with short-wave radios will be able to pick up the BBC World Service (between 24m and 75 m) and the Voice of America.

## RELIGION

The national religion of Spain is Roman Catholicism. Mass is said in almost all churches. In the principal tourist centres, services are also held in foreign languages. Enquire at the tourist office.

## T

## TAXIS

The letters SP (*servicio público*) on the front and rear bumpers of a car indicate that it is a taxi. It will probably also have a green light in the front windscreen or a green sign indicating *libre* when it is avail-

able for hire. Taxis are unmetered in tourist areas. Fares to the most popular destinations are fixed and displayed on a board at the main taxi rank. These are reasonable by European standards. If in doubt, ask the driver before you set off.

| | |
|---|---|
| Where can I get a taxi? | **¿Dónde puedo coger un taxi?** |
| What's the fare to…? | **¿Cuánto es la tarifa a…?** |

## TELEPHONES (teléfono)

The cheapest and easiest way to make any sort of call, from local to international, is in a *Teléfonico* kiosk. You go to a numbered booth, dial the number yourself and pay the person at the desk who has metered your call. Alternatively, you can now dial internationally from any street-corner telephone. Pick up the receiver and when you get the dial tone, dial 07; wait for a second dial tone, then dial the country code, local code (minus the first zero), and then the number you are calling. You will need a plentiful supply of 100 peseta coins. Easy-to-understand instructions in all languages help you.

If you must call home from your hotel (by far the most expensive option), ask in advance how much a 3-minute call will cost.

For national directory enquiries dial **003**; for the international operator (Europe) dial **008**, and for the rest of world dial **005**.

| | |
|---|---|
| Can you get me this number? | **¿Puede communicarme con este número?** |
| reverse charge call (collect call) | **cobro revertido** |

## TIME DIFFERENCES

Spanish time coincides with that of most of Western Europe – Greenwich Mean Time plus one hour. In spring, clocks are put forward an hour, maintaining the one hour difference.

**Summer time chart**

| New York | London | **Spain** | Jo'burg | Sydney | Auckland |
|---|---|---|---|---|---|
| 6am | 11am | **noon** | noon | 8pm | 10pm |

## TIPPING

Since a service charge is normally included in hotel and restaurant bills, tipping is not obligatory. The following are just suggestions.

| | |
|---|---|
| Hotel porter, per bag | 100 ptas |
| Maid, per week | 200 ptas |
| Waiter | 10% |
| Taxi driver | 10% |

## TOILETS

The most commonly used expression for toilets is *servicios* or *aseo*, though you may also hear or see *WC*, *water*, and *retretes*.

Public conveniences are rare, but all hotels, bars and restaurants have toilets, usually of a reasonable standard. It is considered polite to buy a coffee if you drop into a bar just to use the toilet.

## TOURIST INFORMATION OFFICES (*oficina de turismo*)

**Australia**: PO Box A-685, Suite 21a, 203 Castlereagh Street, 2000 Sydney NSW; tel. (02) 264 79 66.

**Canada**: 14th Floor, 102 Bloor Street West, Toronto, Ontario, M5S 1M8; tel. (416) 961 31 31/40 79.

**United Kingdom**: 57-58, St James Street, London SW1A 1LD; tel (071) 499 0901.

**USA**: 665 Fifth Avenue, New York, NY 10022; tel (212) 759-88 22; Suite 960, 8383 Wilshire Boulevard, Beverly Hills, Los Angeles, CA 90211; tel. (213) 658-71 88.

Every town of any reasonable size on the Costa Dorada has its own tourist office, well equipped with maps, leaflets and brochures. The offices at Tarragona and Sitges are particularly good.

## WATER (*agua*)

Tap water is safe to drink, but is not recommended for its taste. The Spanish themselves almost invariably drink bottled water.

| a bottle of sparkling/still mineral water | **una botella de agua con gas/sin gas** |
|---|---|
| Is this drinking water? | **¿El agua es potable?** |

## WEIGHTS AND MEASURES

(For fluid and distance measures see DRIVING on p.124.)

**Temperature**

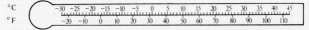

**Length**

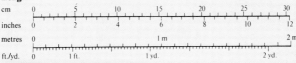

**Weight**

| grams | 0 | 100 | 200 | 300 | 400 | 500 | 600 | 700 | 800 | 900 | 1 kg |
|---|---|---|---|---|---|---|---|---|---|---|---|
| ounces | 0 | 4 | 8 | 12 | 1 lb | 20 | 24 | 28 | 2 lb. | | |

## YOUTH HOSTELS (albergue de juventud)

There are youth hostels at the following locations: **Costa del Maresme**: Cabrera de Mar and El Masnou. **Barcelona**: 5 hostels. **Costa Dorada** (south of Barcelona): El Vendrell, Altafulla, Tarragona, Deltebre. **Inland**: Montserrat, L'Espluga del Francoli. Bed and breakfast costs around 700 ptas for members and 1,000 ptas for non-members. Book in advance.

# Index

Where more than one page reference is given, the one in **bold** is the main entry listed.

# Berlitz – pack the world in your pocket!

**Africa**
Algeria
Kenya
Morocco
South Africa
Tunisia

**Asia, Middle East**
China
Egypt
Hong Kong
India
Indonesia
Japan
Jerusalem
Malaysia
Nepal
Saudi Arabia
Singapore
Sri Lanka
Taiwan
Thailand

**Australasia**
Australia
New Zealand
Sydney

**Austria, Switzerland**
Austrian Tyrol
Switzerland
Vienna

**British Isles**
Channel Islands
Dublin*
Ireland
London
Oxford and Stratford
Scotland

**Belgium, The Netherlands**
Amsterdam
Brussels

**France**
Brittany
Châteaux of the Loire
Dordogne
Euro Disney Resort
France
French Riviera

Normandy
Paris
Provence

**Germany**
Berlin
Munich
Rhine Valley

**Greece, Cyprus and Turkey**
Athens
Corfu
Crete
Cyprus
Greek Islands of the Aegean
Istanbul and the Aegean Coast
Peloponnese
Rhodes
Salonica and Northern Greece
Turkey

**Italy and Malta**
Florence
Italian Adriatic
Italy
Malta
Milan*
Naples, Capri and the Amalfi Coast
Rome
Sicily
Venice

**Scandinavia**
Copenhagen
Helsinki
Oslo and Bergen
Stockholm

**Spain**
Barcelona
Canary Islands
Costa Blanca
Costa Brava
Costa del Sol
Costa Dorada and Tarragona
Ibiza and Formentera

Madrid
Mallorca and Menorca
Seville

**Portugal**
Algarve
Lisbon
Madeira

**Central and Eastern Europe**
Budapest
Hungary
Moscow and St Petersburg
Prague
Yugoslavia

**North America**
Alaska Cruise Guide
Boston*
California
Canada
Florida
Greater Miami
Hawaii
Los Angeles*
Montreal
New Orleans
New York
San Francisco
Toronto
USA
Washington

**Caribbean, Latin America**
Bahamas
Bermuda
Brazil
Cancún and Cozumel
Caribbean
French West Indies
Jamaica
Mexico
Mexico City and Acapulco
Puerto Rico
Rio de Janeiro
Southern Caribbean
Virgin Islands

**144**

* in preparation

029/410 RP